Sacred Cows

Examining the Traditions of Men in the Light of
the Word of God

Rabbi Claude Scheiner

Dedication

This book is dedicated to the glory of Adonai, the God of Avraham, Yitz'chak, and Ya'akov, and His Son, Yeshua, the Messiah and Redeemer of Israel.

It is also dedicated to Carole, my loving wife since 1979, and to our son Sean, the pride and joy of our lives.

Contents

Foreword   IX

Preface   XI

Epigraph   XVII

1. The Traditions of Men   1

2. Mark Chapter 7   5

3. Judaisms   13

4. The Oral Torah and "Fences around the Torah"   17

5. Reinterpreting Messianic Prophecies   25

6. Ritual Conversion of gentiles   29

7. Jewish Genealogy   35

8. The Rabbinic food laws   39

9. The Rabbinic standards regarding Shabbat   43

10. The Roman Catholic church   49

11. The Church Defined   51

12. The Priesthood and the Mass   57

13. Peter and the Papacy   61

14. Fail Mary   65

15. The Confessional   75

16. Purgatory   79

17. The Infallibility of the Pope   83

18. Concluding Thoughts on Catholicism   87

19. Protestantism   91

20. Replacement Theology   95

21. Dispensationalism   101

22. The Status of Gentiles   109

23. Anti-Nomianism   117

24. God's Appointed Festivals   135

25. Man's Festivals linked to paganism   149

26. Holy Cow! What's on the Menu ?   169

27. Tithes and Offerings   195

28. The "Holy Protestant Traditions"   231

29. The Stages of Change   239

30. Concluding thoughts   277

Bibliography and Recommended Reading   279

Author Bio   281

Foreword

In this book, my dear friend and a brother in the faith in Messiah Yeshua, is delving into the heart of the age old conflict between Messianic Judaism, Rabbinical Judaism, and Christianity. Rabbi Claude Scheiner is a great student of the Word of God, a scholar, and a prolific writer. These qualifications give Rabbi Scheiner the necessary tools needed to tackle such a challenging task.

I enjoyed reading every word in this great book and much appreciate the unique way the Rabbi slaughters and dissects the sacred cows.

An eye opener and a must read.

Rabbi Amnon Judah Shor, D. Min.

Bet Shalom v'Emet

Fresno, California

Preface

The purposes of this book are to provide a sure and true foundation for the examination of traditions that have been handed down, sometimes for centuries, to establish criteria for ascertaining the truthfulness of these traditions, and to establish a proper framework to ensure our beliefs and practices are in line with and consistent with the Bible, the written Word of God.

It seeks to fairly represent differing opinions and traditions and to openly compare and contrast those with the Word of God. The goal is not to shame or blame but to reveal the absolute truth. It is about establishing the validity of the content of our faith and practices, something that should be welcomed by all honest seekers of truth.

It is also important to note that this work is not presented as an exhaustive expose and rebuttal of the various issues presented. It is merely an overview of many errors in the traditions of men and seeks to offer reasoned answers from the Scriptures for the various issues being addressed. Each sub-topic is deserving of an entire book to fully examine and explore the issues. That is beyond the scope of this work. That is not to say that an honest presentation and refutation are missing from this work. In fact, many additional resources are listed herein and in the bibliography that invite the reader to dive into the deep end of the pool to find a treasure trove of material and significant scholarly opinions to satisfy a quest for the truth. As is often said, this work stands on the shoulders of giants.

A few words about bias . . .

A bias is an inclination or tendency toward or against a person, group of people, or an idea or opinion. We often use the term prejudice in describing bias. Unfortunately, in so doing, we attribute negativity to the concept. It is possible to have a "positive bias" towards things or people or ideas and opinions. I have a positive bias towards eating healthy foods, at least I try to. I have a natural bias in avoiding dangerous situations or people, if within my control. Bias is ultimately about choosing. It is the basis of that choice that is important. If my choice is based on prejudgment, hasty generalizations, or sloppy research and hearsay, it follows that my conclusions will hardly pass the test of objective scrutiny and will most likely lead me to erroneous and incorrect practices. If I can demonstrate that my reasoning is based on fairly represented objective standards that can be seen as honest and fair, then I can accept that particular bias.

Let me give you a few examples of my personal bias.

I believe that the Bible is the inspired written Word of God. 2 Timothy 3:16,17 states: "Every Scripture is God-breathed and profitable for teaching, for reproof, for correction, and for instruction in righteousness, that each person who belongs to God may be complete, thoroughly equipped for every good work." Here is a passage that establishes the truth that I believe and demonstrates what I have been saying about bias. Many, if not most, Christian commentators claim this verse applies to the so-called New Testament (Matthew through Revelation). It does apply to that also but several issues of bias need to be addressed here. The Apostle Paul (Rav Shaul) is using the term "every" or "all" Scripture. The Greek term "graphe" refers to that which is written. This is important to distinguish this from the Oral Torah. Paul was not asserting that divine authority rests on any so-called Oral Torah. More on this later.

Furthermore, Paul was referring to the only existing written authority in his day, the Tanach, including the Torah. There simply was no other written authority. He was not referring to the gospels or the New Testament; they had not been written down yet! Many modern commentators miss this important point. Do you see how bias works?

Some of my other biases include:

I am a Messianic Jewish believer in Yeshua as the promised Messiah of Israel. I am resolved and fearless in my faith in Messiah, the Hope of Israel.

I believe in the inerrancy of the Bible. This refers to the historical and scientific accuracy of the Scriptures. Hebrews 6:18 and 2 Peter 1:20-21. This means to me there are no discrepancies between the facts of science and the Word of God. There are certainly discrepancies between man's theories about those facts of science and man's theories about the Word of God.

I believe in the infallibility of the Bible. The word infallible simply means not breakable. There exists a divine character of Scripture which necessitates its truthfulness. 1 Timothy 1:15; 3:1; 4:9, 2 Timothy 2:11, 1 Corinthians 7:25.

I believe that the Bible is our absolute standard for the content of our faith and for the practice of that faith. Isaiah 55:10-11, Hebrews 4:12.

My "statement of faith" is actually quite extensive and can be found on my website www.torahforall.org. It is not necessary to reproduce it in its entirety here. The purpose here is to establish some of my bias points which will help the reader understand my approach in addressing and resolving issues and conflicts between the traditions of men and the written Word of God. The actual approach will be addressed in Chapter One.

All Scripture quotations in this book are from The World Messianic Bible. It has also been known as the Hebrew Names Version (HNV) and the World English Bible: Messianic Edition (WEB:ME).

The acronym Tanach or Tanakh is from three Hebrew words: the T represents Torah or the five books of Moses, the N represents Nevi,im or the Prophets and the CH or KH represents Ketuvim or the Writings. These represent the threefold division of what is called the Old Testament.

Yeshua is the Hebrew name that is transliterated as Jesus. Since there is no letter J in Hebrew or Greek and only recently in English for that matter, it is linguistically proper to use the correct name for the Messiah. No one in the first century in the land of Israel heard the letter J pronounced, so names like Jesus, James, or Jehovah are incorrect.

Epigraph

To answer the many questions posed within, I have decided to bypass the usual ivory towers of academia with their theologians who are so skilled at weaving elaborate and lofty, erudite syllogisms, the many axioms of philosophical speculation and the varied postulations that emanate from the advanced mind of man. Instead, I have decided to begin with the ultimate source, the Author and Finisher of our faith, Yeshua, the Messiah of Israel.

Chapter One

The Traditions of Men

It is important to recognize the value of traditions to our culture and to individuals within that culture. Perhaps I should say cultures as we are a rather homogeneous collective of cultures that provide a variety of richness to our overall experience as people. I have been blessed to have been able to travel to and live in many countries. I have been exposed to a variety of cultures, languages, and people groups. The adventure of discovery has always been exciting and illuminating to me personally. That is not to say that all cultural expressions are in line with the Word of God, far from it, but interesting and illuminating, nonetheless.

It is also important to know that my views on traditions are not entirely negative. I have worked in the field of clinical counseling for 30 years and over that time I have seen how long-held traditions can be a source of strength for people, especially in times of crisis. When in fear or pain or a host of challenges, people tend to retreat into their long-held traditions to give them a sense of familiarity and safety. The mere act of "doing" something familiar can bring a sense of normalcy, comfort, and belonging that is especially appreciated during personal challenges.

We actually have some examples of how traditions are viewed positively in the Apostolic Writings, the New Testament.

- In 1 Corinthians 11:2, the Apostle Paul (Rav Shaul) says "Now I praise you, brothers, that you remember me in all things, and hold firm the **traditions**, even as I delivered them to you."

- He also said in 2 Thessalonians 2:15 "So then, brothers, stand firm and hold the **traditions** which you were taught by us, whether by word or by letter."

It is important to recognize, therefore, that the Bible is not hostile to traditions, per se, but as we will see, it does pose some qualifications for traditions to be accepted and practiced.

Perhaps the most grievous error in the history of Israel is that of the incident of the golden calf. It is the recalling of that incident that gave birth to the title of this book, Sacred Cows.

Deuteronomy 9:11- 16 relates the experience of Moshe (Moses) as it states, "It came to pass at the end of forty days and forty nights that the LORD gave me the two stone tablets, even the tablets of the covenant. The LORD said to me, "Arise, get down quickly from here; for your people whom you have brought out of Egypt have corrupted themselves. They have quickly turned away from the way which I commanded them. They have made a molten image for themselves!" Furthermore, the LORD spoke to me, saying, "I have seen these people, and behold, they are a stiff-necked people. Leave me alone, that I may destroy them, and blot out their name from under the sky; and I will make of you a nation mightier and greater than they." So I turned and came down from the mountain, and the mountain was burning with fire. The two tablets of the covenant were in my two hands. I looked, and behold, you had sinned against the LORD your God. You had made yourselves a molded calf. You had quickly turned away from the way which the LORD had commanded you."

Many rabbinical commentaries tend to the idea that, in the making of the sacred calf, the children of Israel did not think they were directly embracing paganism. Many believed that they were using this image as a representative of the true God who did indeed deliver and lead them out of Egypt. As we shall see, however, God does not accept syncretism in worship of Him.

The incident of the golden calf and the subsequent judgments from God should stand as an eternal warning to any who think their embracing of other "sacred cows" could be acceptable to God. Let us not become "stiff-necked" and resistant to the counsel of God. Let us humble ourselves to receive instruction from Him through His Word, the Bible.

Let us now look at some clear examples where the "sacred cow" traditions of men stand opposed and condemned by the eternal, unchanging, and inspired Word of God.

Chapter Two

Mark Chapter 7

I have chosen this example regarding the Bible's instruction regarding traditions because it is the clearest example from the Messiah Himself and establishes the primary principle necessary for the accurate investigation of traditions. I have added some highlights to emphasize some important focus points. I have included Mark 7:1-13 in its entirety to facilitate careful examination.

Mark 7:1-13

"Then the Pharisees and some of the scribes gathered together to him, having come from Jerusalem. Now when they saw some of his disciples eating bread with defiled, that is unwashed, hands, they found fault. (For the Pharisees and all the Jews don't eat unless they wash their hands and forearms, holding to **the tradition of the elders**. They don't eat when they come from the marketplace unless they bathe themselves, and there are many other things which they have received to hold to: washings of cups, pitchers, bronze vessels, and couches.)

The Pharisees and the scribes asked him, "Why don't your disciples walk according to **the tradition of the elders**, but eat their bread with unwashed hands?" He answered them,

"Well did Isaiah prophesy of you hypocrites, as it is written,

'This people honors me with their lips,

but their heart is far from me.

They worship me in vain,

teaching as doctrines the commandments of men.'

"For you set aside the commandment of God and hold tightly to **the tradition of men**—the washing of pitchers and cups, and you do many other such things." He said to them, "Full well do you reject the commandment of God, that you may keep **your tradition**. For Moses said, 'Honor your father and your mother;' and, 'He who speaks evil of father or mother, let him be put to death.' But you say, 'If a man tells his father or his mother, "Whatever profit you might have received from me is Corban," ' " that is to say, given to God, "then you no longer allow him to do anything for his father or his mother, making void the word of God by **your tradition which you have handed down**. You do many things like this."

Now let's examine this carefully and see what we can learn.

First of all, the context is clearly referring to a conflict between Yeshua's disciples and some of the Pharisees. An important second observation is to note that the issue is not about "what" the disciples were eating. This passage has nothing to do with the food laws of Leviticus 11. Had the disciples been eating anything prohibited by the standard of Leviticus 11, that would certainly have been the issue. It was not.

The issue was the fact that the disciples were not adhering to the **"Tradition of the Elders"** regarding ritual hand washing. What was this tradition? There exists a tradition, still extant today, that prior to touching food, the hands must be washed in a specific, ordered way to ensure the foods they touch do not become ritually contaminated, thus rendering them unfit for consumption. The actual process is described in the Talmud, a compendium of the Oral Torah, and is quite elaborate and extensive. The truth is, there is no such requirement in the written Torah[1] addressing such a concern or positing a need for such a remedy. Otherwise clean food, meaning acceptable according to Leviticus 11, does not become unclean merely by the absence of a man-made cleansing ritual. It is the Word of God in Lev 11 that sanctifies and sets apart what may be eaten as food, not the traditions of men!

Yeshua rightly takes them to task for their hypocrisy. He quotes Isaiah 29:13 to illustrate that "their worship of me is useless because they teach man-made rules as if they were doctrines". Yeshua further states, "For you set aside the commandment of God, and hold tightly to **the tradition of men."**

Yeshua goes on to share a parable to illustrate his point.

In Mark 7:17-23 he states the following: "When he had entered into a house away from the multitude, his disciples asked him about the parable. He said to them, "Are you also without understanding? Don't you perceive that whatever goes into the man from outside can't defile him, because it doesn't go into his heart, but into his stomach, then into the latrine, making all foods clean?" He said, "That which proceeds out of the man, that defiles the man. For from within, out of the hearts of men, proceed evil thoughts, adulteries, sexual sins, murders, thefts, covetings, wickedness, deceit, lustful desires, an evil eye, blasphemy, pride, and foolishness. All these evil things come from within and defile the man."

Yeshua is demonstrating the error of the **Tradition of the Elders** regarding ritual hand washing. Biblically approved food, such as outlined in Leviticus 11, does not become unfit for consumption by avoiding man-made ritual hand washing. It is eaten and purged into the latrine.

An important observation is warranted here. Verse 19 includes the words "making all foods clean". First, notice that most honest Bible translators will put that phrase in parenthesis marks or at least have a footnote admitting the truth that those words are not in the original Greek text. They were most likely a side comment added by a scribe that was later added to the text. Even if it is possible that they were originally spoken by Yeshua, it would only further explain the idea that otherwise Biblical foods do not become "unclean" by avoiding the traditional hand-washing ritual.

In Mark Chapter 7, Yeshua contrasts two polar opposites, the authoritative Word of God and the man-made rules of human tradition. When there is a conflict between these two spheres, we must always follow His example and reject any teaching or tradition which does not agree with the Word of God. The principle is just that simple and absolute. I have read several conservative Evangelical commentators who agree with that statement, in principle, but then go on to violate it in their teachings. Unfortunately, many resources are not consistent in their approach to an honest and careful exegesis of Biblical texts.

Yeshua said, "Full well do you reject the commandment of God, that you may keep **your tradition.**" He gives an example of how they circumvent the plain meaning of Scripture regarding the requirement to provide for parents to allow a "legal loophole" to avoid adherence to the command. He charges them as "making void the word of God by your tradition which you have handed down".

Do you see the effect of such a harmful "tradition"? Yeshua states that these traditions were "man-made" and "handed down" to them. These traditions were in conflict with the written Word of God. He knew the danger of allowing people to be in bondage to man-made traditions that, in effect, "nullify the Word of God". The question is, do we know that danger? Are we schooled and grounded enough in the written Word of God to be able to discern the errors of man? Or do we have a theology that simply dismisses the authority of the Word, at least the so-called Old Testament, in favor of a "newer, more relaxed version" of truth? Do we redefine God's absolutes into different times or epochs and different people groups as the modern error of Dispensationalism seeks to do? More on that topic later.

The consequence of pastors and teachers not having examined and protected people from the errors of human traditions that are in conflict with the Bible is the spawn of so many cultic groups, schools of legalism, and serious levels of rebellion and apostasy. Yeshua's words should ring through to today as a clarion call to all believers and especially to all pastors and teachers to ensure you are able to identify and separate out any teaching, opinion, theology, subjective morality, favorite book, favorite tradition, favorite practice or favorite holiday that finds its roots in the false traditions of men, handed down to you that is in conflict with the written Word of God!

---

1. The word Torah is a complex Hebrew word that usually refers to instruction or teaching. It is from the root yareh which is an archery term for "hitting the mark". It is frequently mistranslated as "law". Although the Torah contains "laws" it also contains history, teachings, instructions, poetry, prophecy, and songs.

Chapter Three

Judaisms

I have purposely titled this chapter "Judaisms", in the plural, for a reason. Many people assume that there is and has been one, single, monolithic religion called Judaism that represents a single source of opinion regarding the faith of the Jewish people. A quick review of the Bible or even a trip to a few local synagogues will easily show this to be untrue. There is an old joke about asking a question to three rabbis and you'll get four opinions. Rabbinic commentary and opinions are all over the page. In the case of the Talmud that is literally true where a Bible verse is printed in the center with various and often conflicting opinions surrounding it from different commentators. There is no attempt to resolve the tension. It merely exists to stimulate thought. When the page is turned, a new topic is offered. This method may be confusing and unsatisfying to the modern Western mind and that is part of the point.

Most of us in the modern era look through the lens of a Greek mindset[1] which seeks to reduce everything to a formulaic approach that tries to resolve intellectual tension. In fact, we oftentimes hold so dearly to this approach that we withhold acceptance and obedience to written truth until we have satisfied ourselves as to its meaning and purpose. This kind of bias is dangerous in that we are placing our personal intellectual abilities as the arbiter and judge of the written Word of God. The question becomes, is God and His Word authoritative, or have we become the judge of God? Has God given us the right to withhold adherence to His teachings contingent upon our intellectual understanding, acceptance, and approval?

Consider Abraham, who was raised in paganism and did not have the benefit of a written Bible like we have. He encountered God who revealed Himself to him and gave him great promises of blessing. Abraham was told to follow God and He would give him a land that He would show him. Abraham did not know the actual destination. He did not plug it into his GPS and reason out the waypoints and rest stops. He chose to follow God in faith trusting that his steps would be ordered by the Lord.

The problem with the modern Greek mindset in approaching and understanding the truth of the Bible is that it acts as a barrier rather than an aid. The Hebraic mindset, on the other hand, is not afraid of thinking about options and opinions but it does not use that as an excuse for withholding obedience. It embraces what Marvin Wilson[2] calls "block logic". It does not have to resolve all tensions, in fact, it recognizes that it cannot. That is the essence of humility.

Deuteronomy 29:29 says, "The secret things belong to the LORD our God; but the things that are revealed belong to us and to our children forever, that we may do all the words of this law." In my own personal life, I have many unresolved questions on a number of topics. I have learned to accept the unresolved tension and "leave those on the shelf", so to speak. I will not, however, let those questions and issues prevent me from wholeheartedly following what has been revealed to me.

So now let's take a look at some examples of how Jewish thought has shaped belief systems.

---

1. See Tim Hegg's excellent article entitled "My Big, Fat Greek Mindset" at www.torahresource.com.

2. Our Father Abraham: Jewish Roots of the Christian Faith by Marvin R. Wilson at Amazon.

Chapter Four

The Oral Torah and "Fences around the Torah"

J udaism does have a highly developed code of law. It extends into so many volumes that it makes a fully stocked study look like a lawyer's library. I visited such a study at a synagogue once and it was quite imposing. Where did this come from? This is not the place for an in-depth history of the development of the Oral Torah. For that, I recommend another work[1]. The short version is that the rabbis and sages of Israel determined that the written Torah was not enough. There were too many unanswered questions of halacha[2], the Jewish understanding of how to "walk out" their faith.

These leaders taught that Moses was given the written Torah but also was given an Oral Torah by God. This Oral Torah was allegedly given to include "laws, rules of inference and interpretations". This body of Oral instruction was also allegedly passed down by word of mouth. In the tractate called the "wisdom of the fathers" titled Pirke Avot 1:1 from the Mishnah[3] it is claimed that Moses "transmitted it to Joshua, Joshua to the Elders, the Elders to the Prophets and the Prophets transmitted it to the Men of the Great Assembly. They said three things: Be deliberate in judgment, raise up many disciples, and **make a fence around the Torah**."

In Yeshua's time, it was known as the **Tradition of the Elders**, as recorded in Matthew 15:1-6 and Mark chapter 7. The idea of having an authoritative resource to answer the many questions of how to walk out our faith is understandable. God, however, never endorsed such a concept. Could God have spoken more to Moses than is recorded? Of course! That is probably likely, but it remains to be proven that this was intended to be a source of authority for others.

Consider Noah and his understanding of what God required of him. It is recorded in Genesis 7 that Noah knew the difference between clean and unclean animals which is why he brought a male/female pair of all unclean animals and seven pairs of clean animals into the ark. It is not recorded that God told him this, but it is inferred from his subsequent actions. More on this later.

It is likely that God spoke many things to Adam, Noah, Abraham, Isaac, Jacob, Joseph, Moses, and others that are not recorded in written form. But the Torah itself reveals that God never intended us to govern our lives and interpretations of His

Word by any supposed Oral Torah or to accept word-of-mouth teachings as authoritative. How do we know this?

Deuteronomy 4:2 says: "You shall not add to the word which I command you, neither shall you take away from it, that you may keep the commandments of the LORD your God which I command you." That seems pretty clear and unambiguous. The concept is repeated in Revelation 22:18,19. Both ends of the Bible are consistent in this. It raises the question of why so many modern theologians think it is their job to read the Word of God to you and then proceed to tell you that it does not mean what it plainly says. More on this later.

Deuteronomy 17:14-20 states the following: "When you have come to the land which the LORD your God gives you, and possess it and dwell in it, and say, "I will set a king over me, like all the nations that are around me," you shall surely set him whom the LORD your God chooses as king over yourselves. You shall set as king over you one from among your brothers. You may not put a foreigner over you, who is not your brother. Only he shall not multiply horses to himself, nor cause the people to return to Egypt, to the end that he may multiply horses; because the LORD has said to you, "You shall not go back that way again." He shall not multiply wives to himself, that his heart not turn away. He shall not greatly multiply to himself silver and gold. It shall be, when he sits on the throne of his kingdom, that **he**

shall write himself a copy of this law in a book, out of that which is before the Levitical priests. It shall be with him, and **he shall read from it all the days of his life**, that he may learn to fear the LORD his God, **to keep all the words of this law and these statutes**, to do them; that his heart not be lifted up above his brothers, and that he **not turn away from the commandment to the right hand, or to the left**, to the end that he may prolong his days in his kingdom, he and his children, in the middle of Israel."

It is critical to see that the King of Israel was to write his own copy of the written Torah and govern his life and rule of Israel by it. It was the written Word that God intended to have this level of authority. God never mentioned any so-called Oral Torah as having this level of authority.

In 2 Kings chapters 22 and 23, it was the written Torah, not the Oral Torah, that was the basis of the massive reform led by the godly King Josiah.

In Joshua 8:31-35 we find the following: "Then Joshua built an altar to the LORD, the God of Israel, on Mount Ebal, as Moses the servant of the LORD commanded the children of Israel, **as it is written in the scroll of the Torah of Moses**: an altar of uncut stones, on which no one had lifted up any iron. They offered burnt offerings on it to the LORD and sacrificed peace offerings. **He wrote there on the stones a copy of**

Moses' law, which he wrote in the presence of the children of Israel. All Israel, with their elders, officers, and judges, stood on both sides of the ark before the Levitical priests, who carried the ark of the LORD's covenant, the foreigner as well as the native; half of them in front of Mount Gerizim, and half of them in front of Mount Ebal, as Moses the servant of the LORD had commanded at the first, that they should bless the people of Israel. Afterward, he **read all the words of the law,** the blessing and the curse, **according to all that is written in the scroll of the Torah. There was not a word of all that Moses commanded** which Joshua didn't read before all the assembly of Israel, with the women, the little ones, and the foreigners who were among them.

We learn that in the covenant renewal ceremony performed by Joshua, his source of authority was "that which was written" with no mention of a so-called Oral Torah. Furthermore, it clearly states that "there was not a word of all that Moses commanded which Joshua didn't read before all the assembly of Israel. Not a word that Moses commanded was missing but the source of this was "that which was written". The conclusion is that all that Moses commanded as authoritative was "that which was written", not an Oral Torah.

Another concept that needs to be examined is the idea of creating "fences around the Torah". What does this mean? In the usual sense, a fence is seen as a protective measure or boundary marker. We know where our property line is by means of a fence. We have all heard the quote from the poet Robert Frost, "Good fences make good neighbors". When we live within our boundaries, we are less likely to cause turmoil or harm to our neighbors. The rabbinic understanding of "building fences around the Torah" is a bit different. The sages reasoned that since violation of the Torah was such a significant issue that customs and traditions needed to be established that would protect people from even getting close to violating the actual commands of the Torah. On the surface, the concept appears to have a righteous intention.

The Torah itself addressed a practical side to building fences. Deuteronomy 22:8 states, "When you build a new house, then you shall make a railing around your roof so that you don't bring blood on your house if anyone falls from there." This is a rather practical, common-sense approach to safety. This was obviously to be done to prevent a serious accident from a person falling. The rabbis have extrapolated from this text to imply the need for a fence (tradition) to protect from a "spiritual falling" referring to a violation of the Torah. So many traditions were developed that someone would have to break perhaps a number of traditions before they actually violated the Torah. On the surface, this may make sense and we can't fault the end result ethic they were seeking. However, there are several problems with this approach.

First, it is a direct violation of Deuteronomy 4:2 which prohibits adding to the Word of God. The rabbis would insist that they are not technically "adding" to the Word but merely establishing protective measures to safeguard it. This bit of "wordsmithing" may satisfy some, but the overall effect was the same. The problem is they never stopped adding traditions and safeguards. Furthermore, their traditions were given almost the same authority as the Torah. This has only resulted in adding confusion and ambiguities to understanding the Torah.

Moreover, the issue is compounded by the practice of approaching the Torah and the traditions with a legalistic mindset. This mindset, prevalent in Judaism and Christianity, seeks a "performance-based acceptance" before God. It reduces His Words of gracious instruction to a set of legal and moral codes by which a person seeks to attain and/or maintain their status before God. This is a significant distortion of His Word, and its ramifications include many theological errors that are infecting the body of Messiah to this day. By creating such a treadmill of "works righteousness", the seeker after God is destined to wear out trying to measure up.

Consider two extremes: The person who is not particularly good at "rule keeping", perhaps not out of outright defiance but a simple lack of natural ability. He or she falls by way of giving up and feels depressed, unworthy, and hopeless. Another person is especially meticulous and gifted at adhering to the most intricate minutiae and thereby falls from the sin of pride as he looks down with disdain on those "below him". Neither can find the acceptance they are seeking through such legalism. One falls from guilt, the other from pride.

The fact is, the Torah was never given as a "works righteousness", performance-based document. It was given as God's instructions on how a redeemed people are to live. By perverting the very nature and purposes of the Torah, the rabbis have circumvented God's Word and replaced it with the traditions of men.

---

1. See Chapter Six of "Torah Rediscovered" Fifth Edition by Ariel and D'vorah Berkowitz at www.torahresourcesint ernational.com or Amazon. One of my absolute favorite books.

2. Halacha is related to the Hebrew root for Halach which is the verb which refers "to walk".

3. The Mishnah means "study by repetition". It is an edited record of a complex body of oral traditions.

Chapter Five

Reinterpreting Messianic Prophecies

O ne of the many challenges in dialoguing with Jewish people who do not believe in Yeshua is what they have been
taught regarding what the Scriptures declare about the Messiah.[1] The problem is that the rabbis have not been consistent
or fair in their interpretations of many Messianic prophecies.
Prior to the advent of Christianity, many rabbis correctly iden-
tified many Scriptural prophecies as pointing to Messiah. After
leaders and apologists from within Christianity began to correctly assert these prophecies as pointing to and being fulfilled
in Yeshua, the rabbis backpedaled and reversed course in many
interpretations of Messianic prophecies. This was not done on
the basis of solid scholarship but as a reactionary and defensive
move[2]. During the third and fourth centuries of the common
era, much of the theology from both Christianity and Judaism
can be characterized as "reactionary" in opposition to the "other
side" and not based on careful scholarship. It is much like what

we see in today's hyper-partisan political diatribes from both sides of the spectrum. Truth is frequently a casualty of the war between men, whether theologians or politicians.

It is true historically that during the time of Yeshua and the oppression by the Roman authorities, many Jewish expectations regarding the Messiah were colored by their immediate situation and need for deliverance. These expectations were focused on the immediate return of the kingdom and deliverance from tyranny. Consequently, their focus and expectation were on their need for the promised deliverer, Messiah ben David, the conquering hero as described and prophesied in Daniel 7:13,14 and Zechariah 14:4 and others. We can empathize with suffering people longing for relief in our day as well. We too long for the return of Messiah and the establishment of righteous rule in our world. Come, Lord Yeshua!

The death of Yeshua on the cross seemed to contradict their expectations. They failed to understand the prophecies about Messiah that describe Him as Messiah ben Yosef, the suffering servant of Isaiah 53 and Psalm 22.

This apparent problem was addressed by the rabbis in several ways. First, some Messianic prophecies such as those in Isaiah 53 were reinterpreted to apply to Israel. The context argues strongly against such reasoning, but this interpretation is still prevalent today. Another theory posited that there are actually two Messiahs, one as the suffering servant and the other as the returning conqueror! They could not or would not consider the concept of the same Messiah coming two different times for two different purposes as most of Christianity correctly asserts.

This long-standing theological polarization has resulted in several positions on issues, especially regarding Messianic prophecies, which have become "cemented" in people's minds. It is a serious challenge to break through this level of bias. I believe it can only be done through the power of the Holy Spirit Who reveals truth.

---

1. The word Messiah is from the Hebrew Mashiach and means "the anointed one" who was prophesied to redeem Israel.

2. See the excellent book titled What the Rabbis Know About the Messiah by Rachmiel Frydland on Amazon.

Chapter Six

Ritual Conversion of gentiles

The history of Jewish/gentile[1] relations is not a pretty one, for either side. As is often the case, much of the tension is directly caused or influenced by errant theologies and misunderstandings of passages in the Bible. This section will not be exhaustive of the history and issues for that is beyond the scope of this book. Instead, the focus is on how a specific issue became an issue and what the Bible has to say about it.

How do gentiles become attracted to the God of Abraham, Isaac, and Jacob? It was always the mission of Israel to "be a light to the nations", referring to the gentiles. That light or witness is the Torah of God. This methodology is clearly represented in the famous passage in Deuteronomy 4:5-8 "Behold, I have taught you statutes and ordinances, even as the LORD my God commanded me, that you should do so in the middle of the land where you go in to possess it. Keep therefore and do them; for this is your wisdom and your understanding in the sight of the peoples who shall hear all these statutes and say, "Surely this great nation is a wise and understanding people." For what great nation is there that has a god so near to them as the LORD our God is whenever we call on him? What great nation is there that has statutes and ordinances so righteous as all this law which I set before you today?"

One of the purposes for Israel keeping the Torah was that God gave it to them as the lifestyle of the redeemed. It was (and is) God's instructions for how to live and practice the faith. It is also God's ordained methodology for witnessing. We see in this passage that obedience leads to sanctification which leads to being a witness. As gentiles passed through the land of Israel, they would observe Israel's Torah practices and they would see them as having wisdom and understanding. They would be drawn to the worship of the one, true God. God's purpose for Israel was always to be that light to draw gentiles into a covenant relationship with Him[2].

So, what's the problem with gentiles ?[3] Seen from the Jewish perspective, the issue was simple: idolatry. The gentiles had been steeped in pagan idolatry. They frequently fell back into it, taking Jews with them. It was pagan idolatry that led to the Northern kingdom of Israel being taken into captivity by the Assyrians in 732 BCE[4]. The same thing led to the destruction of Jerusalem and the Southern kingdom of Judah being taken into captivity by the Babylonians in 586 BCE. Idolatry was a real threat. When the Jews returned to the land in the fifth century BCE, the Southern tribes followed the leadership of Nehemiah and Ezra and began a sincere return to the Torah, forsaking any contact with idolatry including contact with gentiles. Unfortunately, this had the effect of marginalizing gentiles. They knew gentiles had significant involvement with paganism and idolatry, so the Jewish leadership "closed ranks" and Israel became an insular community. Prejudice and fear had won.

But what about sincere gentiles who were drawn to the worship of the God of Israel? Was there no path forward for them? The rabbinic answer to the problem of gentiles was to selectively redefine them "as a Jew". Problem solved, right?

The Biblical command to circumcise had always been done as a sign of the covenant[5]. This was creatively misconstrued into an "entrance rite" where a gentile seeking to join in the worship of the God of Israel would undergo it to change his status to that of a Jew. The rabbinic answer is a direct violation of many, many Torah commands regarding the acceptance of gentiles. There is simply no provision or methodology given in the Torah whereby a gentile's status is changed from being an ethnic gentile to being an ethnic Jew. This is an entirely man-made tradition that stands in direct violation of the written Word of God. One clear example is Numbers 15:16 "One law and one ordinance shall be for you and for the stranger who lives as a foreigner with you." If the seeking gentile (foreigner) "became a Jew" then there would be no need to state that the one Torah would apply equally to the native-born Jew and the gentile (foreigner with you).

In later times, about 20 years or so before the advent of the Messiah, the controversy over "what to do with the gentiles" rose to a fever pitch within the Jewish leadership. There is recorded a famous debate and legal battle between two prominent factions within the leadership of the nation, the House of Shammai and the House of Hillel. The end result was the creation of the "Eighteen Measures" which are a complicated list of rulings regarding Jewish/gentile relations and interactions. It placed many restrictions on Jews interacting with gentiles in direct opposition to the Torah. This new theology became a strong religious and cultural prejudice that exerted significant pressure on the Jewish people during the time of the Messiah and the early believers.

We see evidence of this with Peter in Acts 10:28 where we read of Peter's reluctance to even enter the home of a gentile: "He said to them, "You yourselves know how it is an **unlawful thing** for a man who is a Jew to join himself or come to one of another nation, but God has shown me that I shouldn't call any man unholy or unclean." There is nothing in the Torah about restricting a Jew from having fellowship with or entering the home of a gentile. Peter was struggling with the common prejudice of the day that arose from the Eighteen Measures against contact with gentiles. By the way, Acts 10 has nothing to do with food, it is about prejudice against gentiles. More on this later.

The issue of ritual conversion of gentiles became cemented in people's minds. It became accepted theology. The man-made "fence around the Torah" had the force of law. This is the problem with the traditions of men that are in conflict with the Word of God. It has the net effect of nullifying the Word.

---

1. The word "gentile" is a term that merely refers to a non-Jewish person. It is not meant in any derogatory sense.

2. One of my favorite books on this topic is "Take Hold: Embracing Our Divine Inheritance with Israel" Third Edition by Ariel and D'vorah Berkowitz. at Amazon.

3. For an exceptional history of Jewish/gentile relations see the study on Galatians by Rick Spurlock at www.berean sonline.org.

4. The nomenclature BCE stands for Before the Common Era in place of BC and CE stands for the Common Era in place of AD.

5. Another excellent resource is titled "The Letter Writer" by Tim Hegg at www.torahresource.com and Amazon.

Chapter Seven

Jewish Genealogy

I f the issue of Jewish/gentile identification became confusing, then the history of the changing definitions of what constitutes being "Jewish" adds more confusion to our understanding.

There is an inconsistency in the historical definitions of what defines a person as "Jewish". This may surprise some people. After all, there does not appear to be any question or controversy over the ethnicity of someone with various other backgrounds in their pedigree such as German, Russian, Chinese, French, etc. We recognize people with mixed parentage to have an ethnic connection to both sides of their genealogical heritage. In fact, most of us have genealogical connections to many ethnic groups. For example, I am German-Jewish and Irish.

The rabbis have developed a specific definition of being "Jewish" that has changed over time. The current traditional view from the Orthodox community views the term "Jewish" as applying only to a person born of a Jewish mother, defined as "matrilineal descent". This definition, it should be pointed out, is a flip-flop from their definition during the second temple time which was "patrilineal descent", meaning the father's ethnicity was determinative. The Orthodox rabbis today require matrilineal descent, circumcised if male, and not a convert to another religion. They also apply the term "Jewish" to the gentile who undergoes the process of ritual conversion previously mentioned. And so go the traditions of men.

What does the Word of God say about this issue?

According to the examples in the Bible, Jewish descent is based on patrilineal descent (through the father). The covenant was originally made with Abraham and promised to extend through Isaac and Jacob. See Genesis 12:2; 13:16; 15:5; 17:1-2,7; 26:4; 28:14. It was the father who determined the religious identity of his family. After all, circumcision was performed on the males, indicating that the covenant identity applied to the physical descendants of the father.

Some other Biblical examples of patrilineal descent:

- Moses took a wife who was a Cushite and his sons were considered Jewish according to 1 Chronicles 23:14,15

"But as for Moses the man of God, his sons were named among the tribe of Levi. The sons of Moses: Gershom and Eliezer."

- Joseph had an Egyptian wife and yet his sons Ephraim and Manasseh became two tribes in Israel.

- King David was Jewish and yet his great-grandmother Ruth, a Moabitess, and his great-great-grandmother Rahab were both gentiles.

It seems clear from the Biblical witness that the rabbinic tradition regarding determining Jewishness is another tradition of men that is devoid of support and, in fact, contradicted by the Scriptures.

In the final analysis, I suggest the following[1]: Using the framework of the Abrahamic covenant, it is essential to identify both Jews (as Jews) and gentiles (as gentiles) as being together in the covenant of the promise. The enlargement of Israel to accommodate the influx of gentiles was always the plan of God. Israel was to be a light to the nations. Their tent was to be open to seeking gentiles. It is critical to see gentiles being grafted in as a fulfillment of the promise. These seeking gentiles do not "become Jews" through a man-made ritual. They remain as gentiles as evidence of the promise of God. Ephesians 3:6 states" that the

Gentiles are fellow heirs and fellow members of the body, and fellow partakers of his promise in Messiah Yeshua through the Good News".

I Corinthians 7:19, 20 states: "Circumcision is nothing, and uncircumcision is nothing, but what matters is keeping God's commandments. Let each man stay in that calling in which he was called." Since "circumcision" was a way of saying "Jewish", Paul is saying it does not matter if you are a Jew or a gentile. What matters is faith in the Messiah.

Galatians 3:28 states: "There is neither Jew nor Greek, there is neither slave nor free man, there is neither male nor female; for you are all one in Messiah Yeshua." This passage does not negate the facts of actual descendancy of being Jewish or being gentile. There remain distinctions between being Jewish and being gentile just as there remain distinctions of being male or female, despite current societal attempts to blur or remove those distinctions. It emphasizes the spiritual equality between Jewish believers and gentile believers. Our identification is "in Messiah" which makes us part of the "one new man".

---

1. See the excellent book titled, "Fellow Heirs - Jews and Gentiles Together in the Family of God" by Tim Hegg at www.torahresource.com and Amazon.

Chapter Eight

The Rabbinic food laws

One recognizable tradition of Jewish culture is their adherence to certain food restrictions commonly referred to as "kosher" or also "kashrut". In fact, the word "kosher" has entered our common vocabulary to refer to anything that is considered legitimate, legal, or appropriate, such as, "This guy's business dealings aren't exactly kosher." Through common current usage we have come to realize that the status of "kosher" refers to something approved by a recognized authority.

Regarding food, this authority can be two sources, the Word of God or the traditions of men. They do not always agree. The basic Bible definitions of what God has decreed are food are given in Leviticus 11 and Deuteronomy 14. The lists are quite specific and are inclusionary and exclusionary, meaning they list items that are food and those that are not food. Pretty simple and unambiguous, right? Enter the rabbinical opinions and overlays and we end up with a confusing set of rigid rules and definitions.

As an example, let us look at the rabbinic concept of separating meat and dairy. Exodus 23:19 states "You shall not boil a young goat in its mother's milk." This is repeated in Exodus 34:26 and Deuteronomy 14:21. That's all the Word of God says about the matter. The rabbis, however, have extended the meaning to say we are not to eat any meat with any dairy together, so no cheeseburgers or a glass of milk with pot roast. If that were not enough, they say that separate cooking and handling utensils are needed to ensure there is no contact or cross-contamination between any meat and dairy products. Separate dishes and plates are also necessary. Some say that separate refrigerators are necessary to maintain a safe distance. Where does it stop? That is the problem with the traditions of men adding to the Word of God. It never does stop.

Going back to what the text actually says for a moment, there is a specific issue being dealt with and a specific remedy. Let me repeat the text of Exodus 23:19 which states "You shall not boil a young goat in its mother's milk."

In the excellent book titled "Holy Cow! Does God Care About What We Eat?"[1] by Hope Egan, she wisely observes the following regarding the above verse: *"That's it. That's all the Torah says. Nothing else. This command appears in the Torah three times, signaling that God takes it seriously. Thankfully, most of us can easily say that we regularly obey it. Very few of us boil young goats, let alone boil them in milk, let alone boil them in their mother's milk."*

A few comments may shed some light. This command comes within sections of the Torah that deal with the avoidance of pagan practices in the surrounding areas. That may be a clue. There is a theory that the surrounding Canaanite culture, which was thoroughly pagan, used to actually boil a young goat in its mother's milk and use this to bless the fields invoking the name of a pagan god of fertility. Milk as a source of life was perverted into a source of death by this practice. God did not want the Israelites to imitate the pagan practices of the surrounding nations or serve their gods. This is a plausible explanation and fits the context.

Another way to examine if these three texts really teach a complete meat/dairy separation is to see if that interpretation is in harmony with the rest of the Bible. Let us look at Genesis 18:7,8 "Abraham ran to the herd, and fetched a tender and good calf, and gave it to the servant. He hurried to dress it. He took butter, milk, and the calf which he had dressed, and set it before them. He stood by them under the tree, and they ate." Here we see faithful Abraham adhering to the custom of providing hospitality to the three angelic visitors by serving meat and dairy at the same serving. The text says, "They ate". Perhaps Abraham didn't read the rabbinic commentary about separating meat and dairy or perhaps he got it right all along and the traditions of the rabbis are in conflict. I will let the reader judge between the Word of God and the traditions of men.

1. The book Holy Cow! Does God Care About What We Eat? By Hope Egan is a fantastic and thoroughly researched work. It is a filling meal that truly satisfies, is seasoned with grace and served "well done"!

Chapter Nine

The Rabbinic standards regarding Shabbat

B esides the Biblical food laws, the Sabbath[1] is frequently seen as another identifier of the Jewish people. Although not exclusively for the Jews, as we will see in a later chapter, it is almost universally recognized as a practice that does set Jews apart.

To separate out the traditions of men surrounding the Sabbath, it is necessary to first look at the actual Biblical teachings. Here are some clear commands and some related concepts pertaining to the Sabbath that are contained in the Bible.

- Exodus 16:23-29 ... Do not gather (harvest)

- Exodus 20:8-11 ... Remember the Sabbath and keep it holy.

- Exodus 31:13-17 ... Do not work, a solemn rest.

- Exodus 35:2-3 ... A solemn rest, do not kindle a fire.

- Leviticus 23:3 ... A solemn rest, a holy convocation, do no work.

- Leviticus 24:1-9 ... Aaron will arrange lamps, loaves.

- Numbers 28:4-10 ... Additional offerings (lambs, grain/oil/drink)

- Deuteronomy 5:12-15 ... No work, no work for family and servants, all rest

- Numbers 15:32 ... Do not do your ordinary work that you do the other 6 days.

- Nehemiah 10:28-31 ... Do not buy or sell.

- Nehemiah 13:15-22 ... Do not trade, do not prepare to do trade.

- Isaiah 56:2-7 ... Gentiles are included.

- Isaiah 58:13,14 ... Do not do your pleasure – call it a delight.

- Isaiah 66:23 ... Assemble to worship Adonai.

- Jeremiah 17:21-27 ... Do not carry burdens in/out of

your domain.

- Amos 8:5 ... Do not buy or sell.

Why might it be significant that the Sabbath is mentioned at the very beginning of the Bible in Genesis 2:2,3 before there were any people that could be called "Jewish" and before there was a Torah from Moses? Can it be truly said that the Sabbath is just a "Jewish" thing? More on this in a later chapter.

The text in Genesis 2:2,3 states "On the seventh day God finished his work which he had done, and he rested on the seventh day from all his work which he had done. God blessed the seventh day and made it holy because he rested in it from all his work of creation which he had done."

When it says that God rested after finishing all His work, does that imply that He was tired? That sounds silly, doesn't it? What does "rest" mean here? It says that God ceased from His work. The Hebrew word for ceased is "yishbot" and is related to the word "shavat". This is where the term Shabbat comes from. The text tells us that God "ceased" from His work because it was done and complete. He spent the time of Shabbat enjoying His creation. That is the key to understanding how we are to relate to the Shabbat.

God has placed within us the need to have a weekly cessation of our everyday work to simply enjoy the fruit of our labor and to enjoy Him and His provisions for us. God knows that mankind has a strong tendency to keep working, sometimes never stopping to rest. We are designed by God to take a serious break each week. People who violate this principle run the risk of attaining burnout, physically, emotionally, and spiritually.

God also sanctified or set apart the seventh day as that day of rest. This is from sundown Friday to sundown Saturday according to our reckoning of the weekly calendar. Why this time frame? The Jewish calendar has always reckoned the next day starting at sundown based on God's own design shown in the Genesis texts as "there was evening and morning, one day".

So, how have the traditions of man affected our understanding and practices regarding the Shabbat? The rabbis have created a seemingly never-ending list of definitions and prohibitions that make the day anything but a day of rest and grace.

As an example, the Torah does state in Exodus 35:3 "You shall kindle no fire throughout your habitations on the Sabbath day." Is that because kindling a fire involves so much work? I do not think so. I think it reflects the idea of not "creating" since Shabbat is reflective of resting from the prior six days of creating. It is permissible to utilize an existing fire on Shabbat, just not start a new one. Ok, I can accept the simplicity behind this. Apparently, the rabbis cannot. They have determined that starting a car engine on Shabbat is a violation since there is the creation of a tiny spark of electricity that is tantamount to "kindling a fire". In Israel, the elevators have a "Shabbat Mode" that has them stop at each floor going up and going down on Shabbat but not the other days. Why? Because the rabbis have determined that pushing the elevator button makes an electrical connection that is, again, kindling a fire. The same is true for light switches in the home, etc. As an aside, if your electrical switches are prone to "kindling a fire", you might want to consider hiring an electrician. You might have a bigger problem than violating a rabbinic rule regarding Shabbat!

When does it stop? It doesn't. Rules for Shabbat observance exist prohibiting opening an umbrella, running, clipping fingernails, squeezing orange juice, brushing teeth, and braiding hair. Some in the Orthodox community pre-tear toilet paper for use on Shabbat because "tearing" involves "work". Some Karaite Jews even go so far as to avoid going to the bathroom at all on Shabbat because that act itself is considered "work". My opinion is if you have to do a natural bodily function like going to the bathroom and "try" not to until Shabbat is over, THAT is a heck of a lot of "work" that destroys the peace of Shabbat!

In highlighting the above rabbinic concepts, I do not intend to demean the sincerity of religious Jewish people who are attempting to follow a path of piety and obedience to what they believe are requirements that emanate from God. It is simply to show how far the traditions of men have taken their understanding and definitions and how that has created a legalistic treadmill of "works righteousness" that is so opposed to God's grace. It is hard for people who are thus deceived to accurately perceive the grace and mercy of God and His gracious provisions that He created for us to enjoy.

There are many more thoughts about the Shabbat we could delve into and will in a later chapter. The purpose here, however, is to see the simplicity of the Shabbat and get a glimpse of its purpose and gracious provision from our Heavenly Father given to us all for our benefit. Yeshua said in Mark 2:27 "The Sabbath was made for man, not man for the Sabbath." It is a provision of God's grace for our enjoyment and protection, not a device to impose harsh, stringent legalism.

---

1. Shabbat is the Hebrew word for Sabbath

Chapter Ten

The Roman Catholic church

Any attempt to do a full and thorough examination of Roman Catholic doctrine and faith traditions would be a daunting task for the most diligent researcher. The sheer volume of material would humble anyone. That does not, however, deter this author from doing a fair examination and comparison of a few of the most common and recognizable doctrines with the Word of God. After all, we are commanded in 1 Thessalonians 5:21 to "test all things and hold firmly that which is good."

Of the many errors in the teachings of the Roman Catholic church, perhaps the most egregious is the denial of the sufficiency of the sacrifice of the Messiah. They have salvation to sell but it's not free. A heavy dose of human works-righteousness and performance-based acceptance is introduced. The overlay of their teachings ensures that the sinner is always behind in his or her payments. Even after death, a great debt is still owed that must be paid by relatives in the form of payments for masses and prayers for the dead. I will address the heresies of Purgatory and the sacrifice of the Mass a little later.

Perhaps, to the surprise of my readers, there are some points of agreement I find with the Roman Catholic church, such as the doctrine of the triune nature of God and the deity of Messiah. There are, however, many more points of disagreement. As we examine this system of man-made traditions of "pay, pray, and obey", we will focus on the corrective to error found in the eternal Word of God.

As a point of full disclosure, I should also note my personal background with respect to the Roman Catholic church. Although I have a Jewish heritage in my family genealogy, I was baptized, raised and mostly educated as a Roman Catholic. I left the Catholic faith in my early 20s and began a search for absolute truth. After a winding and circuitous route, I became a believer in Yeshua in 1976. This began another quest to pursue truth throughout the many flavors of Protestantism. I finally landed in the Messianic movement in 1999 where I found the firm foundation I was seeking. I was fully ordained as a Messianic Jewish Rabbi in 2013 by Messianic Jewish Rabbi Amnon Shor at Bet Shalom v'Emet[1] in Fresno, California.

---

1. Bet Shalom v'Emet is Hebrew for The House of Peace and Truth.

Chapter Eleven

The Church Defined

What constitutes a "church"? What constitutes "The church"? What does the word "church" mean and where did it come from? These are good questions. They deserve answers.

People are usually surprised when I tell them that "church" is not a Bible word. It is not taken from the pages of Holy Scripture. A rapid-fire response to this statement usually involves getting peppered with many New Testament passages where the word church appears. I am immediately told, "The King James version uses the word "church" 112 times!" What people do not realize is that the word "church" is a word borrowed and used by Bible translators. It is not in the Hebrew or the Greek manuscripts. In the Tanach, erroneously titled the "Old Testament", the Hebrew word that describes the people of Israel is "kehillah". The word means "assembly" or "congregation". In the Septuagint, the Greek translation of the Tanach, circa 250 BCE, the translators used the Greek word "ekklesia", which also means "assembly" or "congregation", to translate the Hebrew word "kehillah". The Greek term "ecc" means "out" and "kaleo" means "call". So, it refers to a group of people who are "called out". So far, so good. The translators show consistency and ac curacy.

Fast forward to the translations of the Apostolic Writings (New Testament) and see what happens. When the translators come across the Greek word "ekklesia", instead of being consistent and using the words "assembly" or "congregation", they insert a new word, "church". Why? I believe it is due to a deeply held bias based on the errors of Replacement Theology that demand they make a distinction between Israel and what they believe is a new body of the people of God. They simply cannot bear the concept of continuity and, therefore, fully embrace the concept of contrast.

So where does the word "church" come from? There is some debate about the origins, but many scholars suggest that its meaning is something that "pertains to, or belongs to the Lord." Even this definition has some bias as it technically can be defined as "pertains to or belongs to a lord", not necessarily The Lord. Do you see how bias works?

So, setting aside the confusion and bias involved in translating, let's see how the Roman Catholic church defines this concept further. What does the word "Catholic" mean and where does that come from? The etymology of the word, according to Merriam-Webster, spans Middle English as "catholik"; Middle French as "catholique"; Late Latin as "catholicus"; and to Greek as "katholikos". Its first known use was not until the 14th century as an adjective meaning "universal" or "general".

So, the Roman Catholic hierarchy assumed the title of "universal" claiming supreme authority on all things.

The actual reality that made the early believers "universal" was their work in sharing the message of the gospel to the whole world. That message was designed for the redemption of the world. What makes any congregation or assembly of believers today truly universal is their faithful adherence to the beliefs and practices of the earliest believers. As will be shown, the beliefs and practices of the Roman Catholic church have deviated significantly from those standards. The later creation of its hierarchy, complete with a sacrificing priesthood, did not fully develop until about five centuries later. In fact, much of what is recognizable today as the practices and traditions of the Roman Catholic church, were developed and added over a span of hundreds of years. This begs the question regarding not only "adding to the Word of God" but also whatever happened to "the faith once for all delivered unto the saints"? There are so many traditions added by the Roman Catholic church that are in direct conflict with the Bible, that more questions arise than can be addressed in this work alone.

When we consider what the foundation of this "assembly" or "congregation" of believers should be, let us consider the following:

- 1 Corinthians 3:11 "For no one can lay any other foundation than that which has been laid, which is Yeshua the Messiah."

- Ephesians 2:20 "being built on the foundation of the emissaries and prophets, Messiah Yeshua himself being the chief cornerstone."

- Ephesians 1:22,23 "He put all things in subjection under his feet, and gave him to be head over all things for the assembly, which is his body, the fullness of him who fills all in all."

Our sure foundation is built on Yeshua, the Messiah, as the Head and built on the Apostles and Prophets. As believers, we are His body. All other later traditions that have been added that are in conflict with this authority have no place in the life of any believer. When we see all the pagan practices introduced during the reign of Constantine, 325 CE, we recognize the level of corruption and error.

Chapter Twelve

The Priesthood and the Mass

Another issue that is central to Roman Catholicism, is the establishment of the priesthood and the Mass.

What is a priest? The Roman Catholic church claims the authority to establish a sacrificing, mediatorial priesthood that assumes the authority to forgive sins against God.

What is the Mass? According to the New York Catechism, "The Mass is the same sacrifice as the sacrifice of the cross." The church teaches that the Mass represents and repeats the sacrifice of the Messiah as "an unbloody sacrifice".

Let us look to the Word of God to examine these issues as it relates to believers in Yeshua.

- 1 Timothy 2:5 states "For there is one God and **one mediator between God and men**, the man Messiah Yeshua."

- Hebrews 7:17, quoting Psalm 110:4, states, referring to Yeshua, "You are a priest **forever**, according to the order of Melchizedek."

- Hebrews 7:24 states "But he, because he lives forever, has his priesthood **unchangeable**." The word unchangeable means inviolate and not transmissible to others.

- Hebrews 7:25 states "Therefore he is also able to save to the uttermost those who draw near to God **through him**, seeing that **he lives forever** to make intercession for them."

- Hebrews 7:26-28 states "For such a high priest was fitting for us: holy, guiltless, undefiled, separated from sinners, and made higher than the heavens; who doesn't need, like those high priests, to offer up sacrifices daily, first for his own sins, and then for the sins of the people. For he did this **once for all**, when he offered up himself. For the Torah appoints men as high priests who have weakness, but the word of the oath, which came after the law, **appoints a Son forever** who has been perfected."

- Hebrews 9:12 states "nor yet through the blood of goats

and calves, but through his own blood, entered in **once for all** into the Holy Place, **having obtained eternal redemption.**"

- Hebrews 9:26 states "But now **once** at the end of the ages, he has been revealed to put away sin by the sacrifice of himself."

- Hebrews 9:28 states "So Messiah also, having been offered **once** to bear the sins of many, will appear a second time, not to deal with sin, but to save those who are eagerly waiting for him."

- Hebrews 10:10-12 states "by which will we have been sanctified through the offering of the body of Yeshua the Messiah **once for all**. Every priest indeed stands day by day serving and offering often the same sacrifices, which can never take away sins, but he, when he had offered **one sacrifice for sins forever**, sat down on the right hand of God."

- Hebrews 10:14 states "For by **one offering** he has **perfected forever** those who are being sanctified."

- Hebrews 10:17,18 states "I will remember their sins and their iniquities **no more**. Now where remission of these is, there is **no more offering for sin**." Messiah's act on Calvary is unrepeatable!

- Leviticus 17:11 states "For the life of the flesh is in the blood. I have given it to you on the altar to make atonement for your souls; for it is the blood that makes atonement by reason of the life."

- Hebrews 9:22 states "Apart from shedding of blood there is no remission." There is, therefore, no such thing as an "unbloody sacrifice."

The Hebrew word for priest is "kohen". In the Septuagint, the Greek translation of the Tanach, this word is translated using the Greek word "hierus". The word "hierus" is entirely absent from the Apostolic writings. There is no such thing as a sacrificing, mediatorial "New Testament Priest" other than Yeshua and as outlined in the Scriptures above, nor is there any need. Yeshua is our High Priest. His sacrifice was **once for all** and is not to be repeated. There is **no more offering for sin**. As Yeshua said from the cross, **"It is finished!"**

Chapter Thirteen

Peter and the Papacy

The Roman Catholic teaching regarding the Apostle Peter is foundational to the authority structure of the Roman church. It is taught, in no uncertain terms, that Peter was the first Pope, that he was given the "keys to the kingdom" representing absolute authority given by Yeshua Himself, and that Peter was the "Rock", meaning the origin of authority and the "head of the church". In the modern symbol for the Pope, one can see the image of the keys clearly represented.

Let us examine the written Word of God to learn the truth. In Matthew 16:15-19 it says, "He said to them, "But who do you say that I am?" Simon Peter answered, "You are the Messiah, the Son of the living God. Yeshua answered him, "Blessed are you, Simon Bar-Jonah, for flesh and blood, has not revealed this to you, but my Father who is in heaven. I also tell you that you are **Peter**, and on this **rock,** I will build my assembly, and the gates of Sheol will not prevail against it. I will give to you the **keys** of the Kingdom of Heaven, and whatever you bind on earth will have been bound in heaven, and whatever you release on earth will have been released in heaven."

In Greek, Peter's name, "Petros", refers to a single rock. The next word for rock in the text is "Petra", which refers to a rock mass or bedrock. The play on words here refers to Peter's confession of Yeshua as Messiah being the bedrock of faith.

In Matthew 18:18-20 the same power is given to the other disciples as well "Most certainly I tell you, whatever things you bind on earth will have been bound in heaven, and whatever things you release on earth will have been released in heaven. Again, assuredly I tell you, that if two of you will agree on earth concerning anything that they will ask, it will be done for them by my Father who is in heaven. For where two or three are gathered together in my name, there I am in the middle of t hem."

The "keys" represent the gospel message all the disciples were to proclaim. Peter did proclaim this in Acts 2:21 "It will be that whoever will call on the name of the Lord will be saved." Peter also proclaimed in Acts 10:42, 43 "He commanded us to proclaim to the people and to testify that this is he who is appointed by God as the Judge of the living and the dead. All the prophets testify about him, that through his name everyone who believes in him will receive remission of sins."

Did Yeshua appoint a fallible man like Peter as the head of His congregation? Peter himself disclaimed such a position as he wrote in 1 Peter 2:4-8 "Come to him, a living stone, rejected indeed by men, but chosen by God, precious. You also as living stones are built up as a spiritual house, to be a holy priesthood, to offer up spiritual sacrifices, acceptable to God through Yeshua the Messiah. Because it is contained in Scripture, "Behold, I lay in Zion a **chief cornerstone**, chosen and precious. He who believes in **him** will not be disappointed." For you who believe therefore is the honor, but for those who are disobedient, "The stone which the builders rejected has become the **chief cornerstone.**"

Paul says in 1 Corinthians 3:10,11 "According to the grace of God which was given to me, as a wise master builder I laid a foundation, and another builds on it. But let each man be careful how he builds on it. For no one can lay **any other foundation** than that which has been laid, which is **Yeshua the Messiah.**"

The foundation is Yeshua the Messiah, not a fallible man like Peter. We see Peter's frailty in faith when he denied that Messiah should be crucified and he received the stinging rebuke from Yeshua in Matthew 16:23 "But he turned and said to Peter, "Get behind me, Satan! You are a stumbling block to me, for you are not setting your mind on the things of God, but on the things of men."

We see the fallibility of Peter again when he denied Messiah in Matthew 26:75 "Peter remembered the word which Yeshua had said to him, "Before the rooster crows, you will deny me three times." Then he went out and wept bitterly."

Once again, after the resurrection, we see Peter struggling with serious error and hypocrisy and was rebuked by Paul in Gal 2:11 "But when Peter came to Antioch, I resisted him to his face, because he stood condemned."

Peter himself, in 1 Peter 1:1 only applies the title Apostle to himself, not Pope: "Peter, an **emissary** of Yeshua the Messiah".

Yeshua is the foundation and cornerstone and the head of His congregation, not a fallible, mortal man like Peter. Colossians 1:18 says "He is the head of the body, the assembly, who is the beginning, the firstborn from the dead, that in all things he might have the preeminence.

Chapter Fourteen

Fail Mary

The Roman Catholic church elevates Mary[1], the mother of Yeshua, to impossible positions of authority. One such title is "Mother of God". God is eternal and can have no mother. He is the creator of the universe and without beginning. Mary was the mother of Yeshua's humanity, not His divinity. Yeshua, as the second person of the triune God, was, in fact, Mary's creator.

The Roman Catholic church also teaches that Mary is some kind of co-mediator along with her Son. However, 1 Timothy 2:5 says, "For there is one God and **one mediator** between God and men, the man Messiah Yeshua". In John 14:6 Yeshua says, "I am the way, the truth, and the life. No one comes to the Father, except through **me**." Hebrews 9:15, referring to Yeshua, says, "For this reason **he** is the mediator of a new covenant". No mention of Mary in any of these verses.

The Roman Catholic church also teaches the Immaculate Conception of Mary. Many Protestants incorrectly think this refers to the virgin birth of Messiah, to which we do agree. The Immaculate Conception of Mary is actually referring to the Catholic claim that when Mary was born, she was free from any taint of original sin. This is a serious error from a Biblical point of view.

- Romans 3:10 says, "As it is written, "There is **no one** righteous; **no, not one**."

- Romans 3:23 says, "For **all** have sinned, and fall short of the glory of God." No mention of an exception for Mary.

- Romans 5:12 says, "Therefore, as sin entered into the world through one man, and death through sin, so death passed to all men because **all sinned**." No exception for Mary.

- 1 Corinthians 15:22 says, "For as in Adam **all die**, so also in Messiah all will be made alive." We all share in the sin of Adam, including Mary.

- 1 John 1:8-10 says, "If we say that we have no sin, we deceive ourselves, and the truth is not in us. If we confess our sins, he is faithful and righteous to forgive us our sins and to cleanse us from all unrighteousness. If we say that we haven't sinned, we make him a liar, and his word is not in us."

To be fair, Mary, herself, never claimed to be without sin. She acknowledged her need for a savior. In Luke 1:46,47 Mary herself says, "My soul magnifies the Lord. My spirit has rejoiced in God **my Savior**". The truth is that only a sinner needs a savior. Mary had a correct understanding of her status as a sinner before God and in need of a savior.

The Roman Catholic church elevates Mary to other impossible places of authority as well. I possess a copy of a book titled "The Glories of Mary" translated from the Italian of Cardinal St. Alphonsus Liguori, founder of the congregation of the Holy Redeemer. It bears the official Imprimatur seal of Archbishop John of New York dated Jan 21, 1852. It is, therefore, officially accepted as Roman Catholic doctrine on the subject of Mary. It lists the following "Offices of Mary."

- Mother of sinners

- Finder of grace

- Securer of pardon

- Giver of perseverance

- Giver of strength
- Protector in temptations
- Helper of dying Christians
- Receiver of her servants at death
- Consoler of the penitent at death
- The destroyer of the serpent
- Mediatrix of salvation
- A loving advocate
- An earnest advocate
- A wise and prudent advocate
- Our peace-maker
- The arbitress
- Saves those for whom she prays
- Helper of souls in purgatory
- Deliverer of souls in purgatory

- Deliverer of those who wear the scapular

- Guide of souls to paradise

- Queen of hell

- Sovereign mistress of the devils

The Glories of Mary also states the following heretical statements referring to Mary:

- "St. Augustine rightly calls her the only hope of us sinners, since **by her means alone** we hope for the remission of sins."[2]

- "St. John Chrysostom repeats the same thing, namely, that sinners receive pardon **only through the intercession of Mary**."[3]

- "He who does not implore **the aid of Mary**, is lost; but who has ever been lost that had recourse to her?"[4]

- "Oh Mary, we poor sinners know **no refuge but thee**. Thou art **our only hope**; to thee we intrust our salvation. Thou are the only advocate with Jesus Christ; **to thee only** we all have recourse."[5]

- "But now, if God is offended with any sinner, and Mary undertakes to protect him, **she restrains the Son from punishing him, and saves him.**[6]

- "Wherefore, St. Bernadine of Sienna says that when Mary, the ark of the New Covenant, was crowned queen of heaven, the power of hell over men was weakened and overthrown." "Oh, how the devils in hell," says St. Bonaventure, "**tremble at Mary and her great name.**"[7]

- "But the point that we here propose to prove is, that **the intercession of Mary is even necessary for our salvation.**"[8]

- "And to increase our confidence, St. Anselm adds, that when we have recourse to this divine mother, we may not only be sure of her protection, but that sometimes **we shall be sooner heard and saved by invoking her holy name than that of Jesus our Saviour.**"[9]

What does the Bible say about all these claims? Is Mary truly the source of grace, the mediatrix of salvation, the source of power from Heaven, the Queen of Heaven and hell, and the valid recipient of worship? Does her exalted position not usurp that of the Messiah Himself?

- 1 Timothy 2:5 says, "For there is one God and **one mediator** between God and men, the man Messiah Yeshua."

- John 14:6 says, "I am the way, the truth, and the life. No one comes to the Father, **except through me**."

- Acts 4:12 says, "There is salvation in **no one else**, for there is **no other name** under heaven that is given among men, by which we must be saved!"

- Ephesians 1:21 says, referring to Yeshua, "far above all rule, authority, power, dominion, and **every name that is named**, not only in this age but also in that which is to come."

- John 10:9 says, "I am the door. If anyone enters in by me, he will be saved, and will go in and go out and will find pasture."

- Isaiah 43:11 says, "I myself am the LORD. Besides me, there is **no savior**."

- Matthew 28:18 says, "Yeshua came to them and spoke to them, saying, "All authority has been given to **me** in heaven and on earth."

- Philippians 2:10 says, "that at the name of **Yeshua** every knee should bow, of those in heaven, those on earth, and those under the earth, and that every tongue should confess that Yeshua the Messiah is Lord, to the glory of God the Father."

- Colossians 1:18 says, "**He** is the head of the body, the assembly, who is the beginning, the firstborn from the dead, that in all things **he** might have the preeminence."

The clear and unmistakable record of the Word of God elevates Yeshua, the Messiah, as the only Savior, the only Deliverer, the only Redeemer Who is our only recourse to give us peace with God and the forgiveness of sins.

---

1. The name Mary is problematic. It is not a Hebrew name. The most likely name for the mother of Yeshua is Miriam.

2. The Glories of Mary, page 83.

3. The Glories of Mary, pages 83,84.

4. The Glories of Mary, page 136.

5. The Glories of Mary, page 130.

6. The Glories of Mary, page 133.

7. The Glories of Mary, page 159.

8. The Glories of Mary, page 170.

9. The Glories of Mary, page 149.

Chapter Fifteen

The Confessional

One of the practices of the Roman Catholic church that deserves attention is that of the confessional. What is the teaching behind it and how does it square with the Word of God? Let's view some primary source teachings to compare with.

The Baltimore Catechism[1]

408. What is confession? Confession is the telling of our sins to an **authorized** priest for the purpose of obtaining forgiveness.

The Catholic Catechism

1456. Confession to a priest is an essential part of the sacrament of Penance.

In the Roman church, it is taught that the priest has the power to forgive all sins committed after baptism. This forgiveness takes the form of absolution by the priest after the penitent privately confesses his or her sins before the priest.

When did such a practice begin? It was not until the year 1215 CE, under Pope Innocent III, that such private confessions were required.

A Biblical response to this practice:

- Mark 2:7 says, "Who can forgive sins but God alone?"

- Acts 8:22 says, "Repent therefore of this, your wickedness, and ask God if perhaps the thought of your heart may be forgiven you." Peter did not hear the man's confession and forgive him.

- 1 John 1:7-9 states, "But if we walk in the light as he is in the light, we have fellowship with one another, and the blood of Yeshua the Messiah his Son, cleanses us from all sin. If we say that we have no sin, we deceive ourselves, and the truth is not in us. If we confess our sins, he is faithful and righteous to forgive us the sins and to cleanse us from all unrighteousness." We confess our sins to God, not to a priest.

- 1 John 2:1,2 says, "My little children, I write these things to you so that you may not sin. If anyone sins, we have a Counselor with the Father, Yeshua the Messiah, the righteous. And he is the atoning sacrifice for

our sins, and not for ours only, but also for the whole wo
rld."

Our Counselor, our Advocate is the Messiah Himself, not a
mere sinful, mortal man like ourselves.

---

1. A Catechism is a religious teaching system using questions
    and answers.

Chapter Sixteen

Purgatory

The word "purgatory" refers to a place and a status. It is believed to be a place of a temporary nature where the soul of the believer is further "cleansed" or "purged" after death before it can proceed to Heaven. Its derivation is from the Latin word "purgatorium", a place of cleansing, from the verb "purgo", meaning to clean or cleanse. This definition and usage imply that the soul of a believer is in need of such cleansing and that individual suffering will accomplish the goal. Both of these ideas are patently false.

- John 5:24 says, "Most certainly I tell you, he who hears my word and believes him who sent me **has eternal life**, and doesn't come into judgment, but **has passed out of death into life.**" A believer simply has eternal life. Now. God only gives one kind of life. Eternal life. He doesn't plan for you to pay for your future sins through your own suffering in a mythical location called Purgatory.

- 1 John 1:7-9 says, "But if we walk in the light as he is in the light, we have fellowship with one another, and the blood of Yeshua the Messiah his Son, cleanses us from **all** sin. If we say that we have no sin, we deceive ourselves, and the truth is not in us. If we confess our sins, he is faithful and righteous to forgive us the sins and to cleanse us from **all** unrighteousness." It is the blood of Yeshua that cleanses us from all sin, not our suffering.

- 2 Corinthians 5:8 says, "We are courageous, I say, and are willing rather to be absent from the body and to be at home with the Lord." This is a binary declaration of our status. We are either in the body (and alive) or absent from the body (at death) and at home with the Lord. There is no room for a third option of Purgatory.

- Rom 8:1 says, "There is therefore **now** no condemnation to those who are in Messiah Yeshua, who don't walk according to the flesh, but according to the Spirit."

- 1 Peter 3:18 says, "Because Messiah also suffered for sins once, the righteous for the unrighteous, that he might bring you to God."

- Heb 10:17 says, "I will remember their sins and their iniquities **no** more."

- John 3:36 says, "One who believes in the Son **has** eternal life."

- 1 John 3:14 says, "We **know** that we have passed out of death into life, because we love the brothers."

- 1 John 5:11-13 says, "The testimony is this: that God gave to us eternal life, and this life is in his Son. He who **has** the Son **has** the life. He who doesn't have God's Son doesn't have the life. These things I have written to you who believe in the name of the Son of God, that **you may know** that **you have eternal life**, and that you may continue to believe in the name of the Son of God."

- Revelation 14:13 says, "I heard a voice from heaven saying, "Write, 'Blessed are the dead who die in the Lord from now on.'" "Yes," says the Spirit, "that they may rest from their labors, for their works follow with t hem."

The teaching of the Roman Catholic church regarding the place of Purgatory as a place where the righteous are "further purged and cleansed" is a complete hoax and fraud. It is perpetrated by the Roman Catholic church to play on fear and guilt and to fleece the flock into paying for masses for departed loved ones to release them from a place that does not exist.

Chapter Seventeen

The Infallibility of the Pope

I nfallibility[1]

NOUN

the quality of being infallible; the inability to be wrong:

"his judgment became impaired by faith in his own infallibility."

(in the Roman Catholic church) the doctrine that in specified circumstances the Pope is incapable of error in pronouncing dogma.

The Vatican Council of 1870 met in Rome and defined the doctrine of the infallibility of the Pope as follows:

"...We teach and define that it is a dogma divinely revealed that the Roman Pontiff when he speaks Ex Cathedra, that is, when in discharge of the office of pastor and doctor of all Christians, by virtue of his Apostolic authority, he defines a doctrine regarding faith and morals to be held by the universal Church, by the divine assistance promised him in blessed Peter, is possessed of that **infallibility** with which the divine Redeemer willed that His Church should be endowed for defining doctrines regarding faith and morals and that therefore such definitions of the Roman Pontiff of themselves – are not by virtue of the consent of the Church – are **irreformable**. But if anyone – which may God forbid! - presume to contradict this our definition; let him be anathema."

So there we have the official definition. Whatever the Pope determines regarding anything pertaining to faith or morals is absolute, guaranteed true, not open to discussion or debate, forced upon the Church with or without their consent, and, most importantly, irreformable. With this last word "irreformable" the Roman church has literally painted itself into a corner. If the Pope speaks for the church, can't be wrong, and can't change his mind, then, by definition, the Church can never repent, even if shown error.

I remember as a young man that the Roman Catholic church taught that eating meat on Friday was a mortal sin. It was a serious restriction that our family followed scrupulously. Then in 1966, that changed; Vatican II changed the rules. This was troubling to me and others. How can the church "change"? What did this mean for other teachings that were supposed to be absolute and unchangeable? What happened to all those poor departed souls who went to hell on a meat rap? Were they retroactively pardoned? The whole authority structure began to appear rather shaky. I would later learn that I was not alone in my uncertainty about the "sure foundation" of the Catholic faith. A few small pebbles of "change" started a landslide in the minds of many.

I left the Catholic church in the early 70s, not because of any single issue, but due to a growing awareness and understanding of the Catholic church's arrogance, domineering attitude towards dissent, abusive control of its members, questionable theological assumptions and conclusions, links to pagan practices and outright dishonest and deceptive claims. My rejection, at this point, was not based on any solid Scriptural background. As a typical Catholic, I was Biblically ignorant. My grounding in Biblical understanding came later. I simply held up the claims of the Roman Catholic church in the light of logic, fairness, and the examination of the fruit of their teachings. They clearly failed the test. My quest for truth continued in my pursuit of learning through the various schools of Protestantism which is the topic of later chapters.

---

1. As defined in www.dictionary.com

Chapter Eighteen

Concluding Thoughts on Catholicism

As I previously stated, I recognize and appreciate any truth that the Roman Catholic church teaches that accords with the written Word of God such as the inspiration of the Bible, the triune nature of God, the virgin birth, deity, and the bodily resurrection of Messiah, etc.

The Roman Catholic church may, indeed, teach the inspiration of Scripture but, much like the Pharisees we previously read about in Mark 7, they nullify the written Word by their traditions. Their added body of human traditions of men has much the same authority as the written Word and is frequently at odds with it.

The Roman Catholic church may, indeed, teach the deity of Messiah and His accomplishments on the cross that resulted in the forgiveness of sins, however, they put Mary, saints, and priests as intercessors and mediators between God and man. It interposes a complex system of works-righteousness and a sacrificing priesthood thus nullifying the once for all sacrifice of Yeshua. It supplants the authority of Messiah as "Head of the Church" with a man as an infallible pope with absolute power to whom obedience is mandated on pain of excommunication and loss of the hope of eternal life.

Cardinal Newman, in his book, "The Development of the Christian Religion,"[1] admits that ... "Temples, incense, oil lamps, votive offerings, holy water, holidays and season of devotions, processions, blessing of fields, sacerdotal vestments, the tonsure (of priests and monks and nuns), images ... **are all of pagan origin...**"

When one studies the history of the Catholic church and especially the lives and conduct of the popes, it becomes apparent that we are certainly dealing with fallible men who made mistakes, changed their positions, were on either side of many issues, including scientific[2] ones, and often led lives that do not reflect any recognizable level of humility, piety or sanctification.

Is it any wonder that when the Catholic church ruled the world, it was called the "Dark Ages"?

---

1. An Essay on the Development of Christian Doctrine by Cardinal John Henry Newman, 1845.

2. Galileo was condemned for heresy by both Pope Paul V (1605-1621) and Pope Urban VIII (1623-1644) for holding a true scientific theory supporting Copernican heliocentrism, the idea that the earth revolves the sun. This teaching was in contrast to official church teaching!

Chapter Nineteen

Protestantism

In the 1970s, as a former Roman Catholic seeking truth, I was certainly handicapped by my ignorance of the Word of God. I had no objective standard of truth to help me navigate the dizzying array of "spiritual" options available to me. To make matters worse, I was not yet a "believer" in Bible terms. As a Catholic, I had been "religious" but never had a "relationship" with God. There is a profound difference.

I have never been an "atheist". Simply from a philosophical perspective, I have always rejected this position. Atheism takes as its premise the absolute fiat statement, "There is no god." Aside from being arrogant and somewhat prideful, it's oxymoronic in "proving a negative".

Someone once said that an atheist is "a person with no invisible means of support."

I have always believed in a Creator Who sustains and cares for this world and its inhabitants, although my Catholic upbringing distorted my understanding and added much in the way of fear and guilt. It was then, in 1976, that I read a book that I consider "an avalanche of Truth". The book was Evidence That Demands a Verdict by Josh McDowell. I was genuinely impressed at the sheer volume and scholarly depth of the material as it led me to a deeper understanding of the authority and reliability of the Bible, explained what constitutes real faith, and showed what a true relationship with God through His Son, Yeshua, looks like. I accepted Yeshua as my Lord and Savior and thus began my spiritual journey through the land of Protestantism.

Due in large part to my ignorance of what different Protestant churches taught, I was understandably confused for a while. It seemed that each different church had quite a different spin on various Scriptures and practices. It reminded me of going to an ice cream shop that offered 37 flavors, although, in this case, there were hundreds. I wasn't trying to be legalistic or prideful, I just wanted to understand the Bible as a whole unit and a continuous revelation, which is what I perceived it to be.

The Apostle Peter gives us an important piece of wisdom regarding understanding the writings of the Apostle Paul in 2 Peter 3:15-16, "Regard the patience of our Lord as salvation; even as our beloved brother Paul also, according to the wisdom given to him, wrote to you, as also in all of his letters, speaking in them of these things. In those, there are **some things that are hard to understand**, which the **ignorant and unsettled**

twist, as they also do to the other Scriptures, to their own destruction." Peter is giving us a word of caution regarding how challenging it can be to always understand the writings of Paul correctly. This makes sense when you understand Paul's extraordinary scholastic background. He was quite learned in not only the Torah but also the Oral Torah and in the Midrashim (interpretations) and skilled at debating. He was fluent not only in his native language of Hebrew but also in Greek. He was trained at the feet of Gamli'el at his yeshiva (house of study). Gamli'el was the grandson of the famous Hillel, a Pharisee and one of the leaders of the Sanhedrin. For Paul, studying under him was the equivalent of clerking for one of the justices of the U.S. Supreme Court.

There is an old joke about Paul . . .

"How will we recognize the Apostle Paul when we get to Heaven?" The answer is, "He's the one wearing the T-shirt that says, 'But, I never said that!'"

Two of the most common errors prevalent today, based on misunderstanding Paul, are the teachings known as Replacement Theology and Dispensationalism. I will address them separately.

Chapter Twenty

Replacement Theology

The theology called Replacement Theology, also often called Supersessionism, teaches that the nation of Israel, as God's covenant people, has been replaced or superseded by the entity called "the church". This teaching also claims that much of the Old Testament has been done away with, including the promises of the Millennial Kingdom of Messiah ruling in Jerusalem and the restoration of Israel. In order to make the words of the Bible fit this preconceived outcome, the approach to interpreting the Bible involves the frequent application of allegory where the literal meaning of the words on the page gives way to a "deeper" or "spiritual" meaning. The problem with this bias in interpreting the Scriptures is that there are literally no limits on where this apriori assumption can take you. There remains no objective word that can stop the runaway train from injecting any meaning into a text under scrutiny. In a theologically borderless world, anything goes. So, the seventh day of Shabbat is redefined as Sunday. The festivals of Leviticus 23 are ignored, and new festivals are added. Baptism is misapplied as an entrance rite for infants. Any blessings from God found in the pages of the Old Testament are claimed for the church. Any curses left therein belong to the Jews.

This approach frequently uses the phrase "New Covenant" in its defense. It is a useful catch-all phrase that is meant to deflect any and all criticism of the theology by asserting that since God has replaced Israel with the church under a New Covenant, the Old Covenant with Israel has been done away with. There are a lot of problems with this approach.

What is the New Covenant?

When we examine what the text actually says, instead of what the theologians tell us what the text means, we find some interesting things. The New Covenant, as it is called, is revealed in Jeremiah 31:31-37. "Behold, the days come," says the LORD, "that I will make a new covenant with **the house of Israel**, and with **the house of Judah**, not according to the covenant that I made with their fathers in the day that I took them by the hand to bring them out of the land of Egypt, which covenant of mine they broke, although I was a husband to them," says the LORD. "But this is the covenant that I will make with **the house of**

Israel after those days," says the LORD: "I will put **my law** in their inward parts, and I will write it in their heart. I will be their God, and they shall be my people. They will no longer each teach his neighbor, and every man teach his brother, saying, 'Know the LORD;' for they will all know me, from their least to their greatest," says the LORD, "for I will forgive their iniquity, and I will remember their sin no more." The LORD, who gives the sun for a light by day, and the ordinances of the moon and of the stars for a light by night, who stirs up the sea, so that its waves roar— the LORD of Hosts is his name, says: "If these ordinances depart from before me," says the LORD, "**then** the offspring of Israel also will cease from being a nation before me forever." The LORD says: "If heaven above can be measured, and the foundations of the earth searched out beneath, **then** I will also cast off all the offspring of Israel for all that they have done," says the LORD."

This passage teaches many fundamental truths about the New Covenant. First, it should be pointed out that the Hebrew word for new is "chadash" which can also mean renewed. It is used this way referring to the "new" or "renewed" moon each month. In fact, the word for month, in Hebrew, is "chodesh", from the same root. So, the covenant Jeremiah is referring to can be referred to as a covenant renewal. This is important when we consider the recipients of this renewal. The text clearly states this covenant is to be with **the house of Israel** and **the house of Judah**. This prophecy was written during a time when the northern kingdom of Israel had been dispersed in judgment with only the kingdom of Judah left in the land. This prophecy of a future restoration demonstrates God's gracious intent to have both kingdoms present as recipients.

Second, there is no mention of a "replacement" group of people called "the church". What is different is not the people group but the many provisions of this renewed covenant. The text informs us that this covenant will be different from the previous covenant. What is this difference?

God says that He will write His Torah on their hearts. Far from a "new" Torah, it is His Torah, the one and only Torah, that He will internalize in people's hearts. He will provide a divine enablement to walk in His ways, as outlined here in Jeremiah 31 and Ezekiel 36. This provision of writing the Torah on the hearts of the people is not a new promise. It was promised in Deuteronomy 30:14 and referred to in 1 Corinthians 2:16.

- The Lord will be their God in fulfillment of Exodus 6:7 and Ezekiel 37:27.

- Israel and Judah shall be God's people.

- They shall all know the Lord.

- God will forgive their sin.

- God will regather the people of Israel to their land.

- God will spiritually cleanse Israel.

- God will give the nation a new heart.

- God will put His Spirit within them.

- They will be faithful to the covenant of the Torah.

According to Jeremiah 31:35-37, since the sun, moon, and stars are still in existence and since the heavens can't be measured and the foundations of the earth have not been searched out, we can conclude that God has NOT done away with or replaced Israel.

- The Apostle Paul concurs as he writes in Romans 11:1, "I ask then, did God reject his people? May it never be!"

- In Romans 11:26 he states, "And so all Israel will be saved."

- In Romans 11:28, 29 he further states. "Concerning the Good News, they are enemies for your sake. But concerning the election, they are beloved for the fathers' sake. For the gifts and the calling of God are irrevocable."

The Apostle Paul did not believe in so-called Replacement Theology, and neither should we.

Chapter Twenty-One

Dispensationalism

T he other creation of the theologians is a relatively new one. Many Protestants I talk to who belong to this camp are surprisingly uninformed about it. It is not uncommon to hear Bible teachers describe different "dispensations" or "time periods" of how God deals with people here on planet Earth. This scheme of dividing the Word of God according to epochs of differing approaches by God to solving the problem of man's sin and redemption is actually a young one in the history of theological "traditions of men". It is only a few hundred years old! Consider the ramifications of anything "new" in terms of "the faith once delivered unto the saints". Can anything "new" actually be "true"? Just a question to ponder.

If we accept the premise that God does not change (i.e. that He is the same yesterday, today, and forever) and also that "The Faith" was "once for all delivered" then there can be no "new gospel".

All God's truth is ancient.

C.H. Spurgeon said:

"There shall be no new God, nor new devil, nor shall we ever have a new Saviour, nor a new atonement. Why then should we be attracted by the error and nonsense which everywhere pleads for a hearing because they are new? To suppose the Theology can be new is to imagine that the Lord himself is of yesterday. A doctrine lately true must of necessity be false. Falsehood has no beard, but truth is hoary with age immeasurable. The old Gospel is the only Gospel. Pity is our only feeling toward those young preachers who cry: 'See my new Theology!' in just the same spirit as little Mary says: 'See my pretty new frock!'"

Dispensationalism was created as a reaction to what was perceived as error with the first approach, that of Replacement Theology. Instead of having Israel totally replaced by the entity called the church, this new view sought to return to a more authentic grammatical, historical interpretation of the Bible. At least, that was the theory. This approach to understanding Scripture, however, is predicated on the rigid assumption that all interpretations must adhere to the requirement to completely separate any and all references between Israel and the church. The approach begins with this unflinching bias and thereby distorts the understanding of many Scriptures. This system divides the Word of God into different time periods where, essentially, the rules are different. It is taught that there was a linear period of time they call Law that was suspended to allow for the next time period called Grace. Accordingly, we are, therefore, now in the age of grace or the church age. According to this "tradition of men", after the supposed rapture of the church, God will again resume the age of Law with Israel.

Many problems are spawned by this error in thinking. It assumes that God changes His mind. Do we not understand that He "changes not" and that "He is the same, yesterday, today and forever"? See Hebrews 13:8, Malachi 3:6, James 1:17, Numbers 23:19, Isaiah 40:8, Psalm 102:25-27, 2 Tim 2:13, Isaiah 40:28, Psalm 119:89, Psalm 33:11, Psalm 90:2, Psalm 119:90, 1 Tim 1;17, to name a few.

One question to ponder is if, despite all the references just mentioned, you still believe that God does change, consider the ramifications to your current pet theology. For the sake of argument, let's say God had Plan A, called Law. Since that didn't work out, He created Plan B, called Grace. What would prevent God from reaching a point where He decides that, in His opinion, Plan B, called Grace, wasn't working out to meet His expectations so He decides to change again and come up with Plan C, something totally different yet? I know this line of reasoning sounds silly and it is but that is the point, is it not? God does not change. Period.

The other problem with this false bifurcation of the Word of God is that it completely separates Law (meaning Torah or instruction) from Grace as if His teaching could be against His grace or the other way around. It forces the conclusion that there "was no Grace in the Old Testament" a preposterous argument. It also equally asserts there is no Law (teaching) in the New Testament.

Consider a very partial list of the Scriptures that speak of God's grace in the Tanach "Old Testament":

- Genesis 6:8

- Genesis 12:3

- Genesis 50:20

- Exodus 4:12

- Judges 10:16

- Joshua 2:11

- Psalm 51:1

This false assumption regarding law and grace finds its way into Bible translations as well. Consider John 1:17. The King James translation has it "For the law was given by Moses **but** grace and truth came by Jesus Christ." The translators have inserted the word **but** in the text. The fact is it is not in the Greek text and most modern translators have corrected this error. By adding the simple word *"but"* within the sentence, the entire sense is changed from one of **continuity** where the promise of grace and truth by Moshe is realized in Yeshua, to that of **contrast** which separates law from grace. This is only one example of how bias in translation can have profound effects on our understanding of the Word of God.

Let us examine what the Scriptures themselves clearly teach and submit our theology to that as the final and absolute determiner of truth.

Consider the commentary provided by the Messiah Himself. In John 10:16 He states "I have other sheep which are not of **this fold**. I must bring them also, and they will hear my voice. They will become **one flock** with **one shepherd**." He is speaking with His Jewish disciples, those who are of "this fold". He is telling them that there are other sheep not from "this fold", meaning gentiles. These believing gentiles are to be **brought in** with the goal of having **one flock** with **one shepherd**. Do you see the unity pictured here? Not one flock replacing the other flock as in Replacement Theology. Not two flocks as in Dispensationalism. One flock with one shepherd.

Consider the Apostle Paul and his teaching in Romans 11. He uses the olive tree as his teaching example of how this relationship between Israel and the gentiles works. Rather than replacing Israel or setting it aside, he sees a single tree into which gentiles are grafted in.

Replacement theology would picture it differently. It would cut down the olive tree (Israel) and plant a new tree (the church, the New Israel) in its place.

Dispensationalism would picture it differently. It would leave the olive tree standing where it is, ignore it, and plant a new tree (the church) next to it.

Dispensationalism is the modern, errant theological invention based entirely upon the traditions of men that spawned the relatively recent errant teaching of the "pre-tribulation rapture of the church". The pre-tribulation rapture theory is the fruit of the poisonous tree of Dispensationalism and should be rejected in total. It is teaching not supported by the Scriptures but by a twisted hermeneutic that ignores context and represents a significant distortion of the teaching of the Word of God.

The Apostle Paul would cringe at these misrepresentations of his otherwise clear teaching picture. He described these believing gentiles not in terms of replacement or something new and separate but actually "grafted in" to the **same olive tree** and sharing in the same richness. It is the perfect illustration of Jews and gentiles together as a foreshadowing of the final salvation when Paul says "All Israel will be saved."

Chapter Twenty-Two

The Status of Gentiles

The entire book of Ephesians is all about the believer's identity in the Messiah. In counseling sessions with people struggling with identity issues or depression, I often "prescribe" a regular and frequent "dose" of the entire book of Ephesians. Herein we learn we are chosen, adopted, forgiven, redeemed, sealed, and have assurance. For those who respond well to "daily affirmations", it is a rewarding place to invest some time and reflections.

Let's look at the text in Ephesians chapter 2 and see what is revealed regarding believing gentiles. I have included the chapter in full with some highlights as focus points prior to the comments.

"You **were** made alive when you **were** dead in transgressions and sins, in which you **once** walked according to the course of this world, according to the prince of the power of the air, the spirit who now works in the children of disobedience. We also all **once** lived among them in the lusts of our flesh, doing the desires of the flesh and of the mind, and **were** by nature children of wrath, even as the rest. But God, being rich in mercy, for his great love with which he loved us, even when we **were** dead through our trespasses, made us alive together with Messiah—by grace you have been saved— and raised us up with him, and made us to sit with him in the heavenly places in Messiah Yeshua, that in the ages to come he might show the exceeding riches of his grace in kindness toward us in Messiah Yeshua; for by grace you **have been** saved through faith, and that not of yourselves; it is the gift of God, not of works, that no one would boast. For we are his workmanship, created in Messiah Yeshua for good works, which God prepared before that we would walk in them. Therefore remember that **once** you, the **Gentiles** in the flesh, who are called "uncircumcision" by that which is called "circumcision" (in the flesh, made by hands), that you **were** at that time **separate from Messiah, alienated from the commonwealth of Israel**, and **strangers from the covenants of the promise,** having **no hope** and **without God** in the world. **But now** in Messiah Yeshua you who **once were far off** are **made near** in the blood of Messiah. For he is our peace, who **made both one**, and broke down the middle wall of separation, having abolished in his flesh the hostility, the law of commandments contained in ordinances[1], that he might create in himself **one new man of the two**, making peace, and might reconcile them both in one body to God through the cross, having killed the hostility through it. He came and preached peace to you who **were far off** and to those who were near. For through him, we both have our access in one Spirit to the Father. So then you are **no longer strangers and foreigners**, but you are **fellow citizens with the holy ones and of the household of God**, being built on the foundation of the emissaries and prophets, Messiah Yeshua himself being the chief cornerstone; in whom the whole building, fitted together, grows into a holy temple in the Lord; in whom you also are built together for a habitation of God in the Spirit."

Ephesians 3:1-7 continues the thought, "For this cause I, Paul, am the prisoner of Messiah Yeshua on behalf of you Gentiles, if it is so that you have heard of the administration of that grace of God which was given me toward you, how that by revelation the mystery was made known to me, as I wrote before in few words, by which, when you read, you can perceive my understanding in the mystery of Messiah, which in other generations was not made known to the children of men, as it has now been revealed to his holy emissaries and prophets in the Spirit, that the **Gentiles** are **fellow heirs** and **fellow members of the body**, and **fellow partakers of his promise** in Messiah Yeshua through the Good News, of which I was made a servant according to the gift of that grace of God which was given me according to the working of his power."

This is a powerful text that speaks specifically to gentile believers and to their place in the kingdom of God. I highlighted certain words to emphasize the **past tense** nature and the **present tense** after coming to faith.

Before

- Were dead in transgressions and sins.

- Once walked according to the course of this world.

- Once lived in the lusts of your flesh.

- Were by nature children of wrath.

- Were dead through your trespasses.

- Separate from Messiah.

- Alienated from the commonwealth of Israel.

- Strangers from the covenants of God's promise.

- In this world without hope.

- Without God.

- Once "far off".

After

- Were made alive.

- By grace, you have been saved.

- Raised up with Him.

- Made to sit with Him in the heavenly places.

- His workmanship.

- Have Messiah.

- Made us both one.

- Fellow heirs.

- Fellow members of the body,

- Fellow partakers of His promise in Messiah.

- Fellow citizens of the holy ones and of the household of

God.

- No longer foreigners and strangers.

- Have hope.

- Members of God's family.

- Now "brought near".

In establishing the truth of how believing gentiles are grafted into the flock of believing Jews, it is important to understand this in terms of what is called progressive revelation. These statements by Paul to the Ephesians are not to be understood as a change in God's overall plan, as previously refuted, but quite the opposite. There is **continuity** represented here as opposed to **contrast**. God's plan for the redemption of mankind has always envisioned a place for gentiles alongside Jews. It goes all the way back to the Abrahamic covenant and even before.

In Ephesians 3:2 Paul refers to "the administration of that grace of God which was given me toward you" and "how that by revelation the **mystery** was made known to me". What is this mystery Paul was talking about? The key to understanding is found in his next statement "The **mystery** of Messiah, which in other generations **was not made known** to the children of men, **as it has now been revealed** to his holy emissaries and prophets in the Spirit". This mystery is not the creation of something new or a change in God's preordained plan. The word mystery refers to something not previously revealed to those generations but now is revealed to this generation. The death, burial, and resurrection of the Messiah were preordained by God before the creation of the world. His desire and plan to redeem mankind had already been established in God's mind. What Paul says is now revealed is "that the Gentiles are fellow heirs and fellow members of the body, and fellow partakers of his promise in Messiah Yeshua through the Good News". Paul further describes this as "the mystery which for ages has been hidden in God". Moreover, Paul further states "that now through the assembly the manifold wisdom of God might be made known to the principalities and the powers in the heavenly places".

Paul is giving an example of progressive revelation of a previously established fact, namely, God's overall plan of salvation which always envisioned the inclusion of gentiles alongside Jews through faith in the atoning sacrifice of the Messiah.

---

1. The Greek word for "dogma" always refers to man-made traditions, likely the traditions of men, the Oral Torah, not the Written Torah.

Chapter Twenty-Three

Anti-Nomianism

Well, there's a fancy word. It's a useful word to whip out to impress people at your next Bible study. Actually, it emanates from the Greek "anti" meaning "against" and "nomos" meaning "law". In the general sense it can mean "against law" or "lawlessness". This usage, unfortunately, has quite a broad application in our current society.

Our focus is on the religious understanding of the term. The word "nomos", is the Greek word used to translate the Hebrew word "torah" in the Tanach, called the Old Testament. The word "torah" is a complex word that has various definitions, all context-dependent. In most cases, the Torah refers to the first five books of the Bible, Genesis, Exodus, Leviticus, Numbers, and Deuteronomy. These are also referred to as the "books of Moshe or Moses" since he wrote them. Another title is the word "Chumash[1]" for the first five books of the Hebrew Bible. In a broader sense, the word "torah" simply means "teaching" or "instruction".

The translators who gave us the Septuagint[2], which is the Greek translation of the Hebrew Scriptures, used the word "nomos" to translate the Hebrew word "torah" since that word was unique to Hebrew. It was an attempt to provide an equivalency in the minds of the readers to facilitate understanding. By use of this word, however, it inadvertently introduced the word "law" in their minds since that is the usual meaning of the Greek word "nomos". They would have been better served to simply transliterate the word "torah" into Greek to maintain the unique distinction in the minds of the readers.

Words can be powerful things. When we hear the phrase "the Old Testament" the word "old" jumps off the page at us. We think through our current filters and immediately connect "old" with an antique, perhaps something worthy of sitting on the shelf but not to actually use. It is an artifact from the past from a bygone era, a part of history that belongs in a museum.

When we hear the phrase "the New Testament" the word "new" also telegraphs meaning and definition to us. "New" must mean something current, up-to-date, applicable now, the latest and greatest, and the attainment or pinnacle of accomplishment. This would certainly supersede the "old", right? Wrong.

These are unfortunate word choices to describe the eternal Word of God. Nowhere do the Scriptures bifurcate themselves with these labels and place an artificial separation page within. The theologians and the Bible publishers are to blame for that. The Word of God is one continuous revelation of His will and teaching for us. There is perfect continuity, not false contrast, within the stream of progressive revelation from the beginning of Genesis to the end of Revelation.

The unfortunate word choice misrepresenting the Torah is the word "law". Certainly, the Torah does contain some laws, known as statutes or ordinances. God never envisioned a lawless society for mankind, despite mankind's ever-increasing movement in that direction. The Torah also includes history, teaching, poetry, guidance, instruction, correction, important genealogical tables, promises from God, and much more. To define this broad category by the limiting word "law" creates a false impression and leads to false conclusions regarding its many purposes.

So why do so many Christians have a problem with "the law"? There is a widely held tradition that says that since we are "saved by grace and not by works" and that we are "not under the law" we have no relation to that law. This traditional interpretation is so common that in discussing the issue, it is an automatic reflexive, knee-jerk response from most Christians including pastors and teachers. It is as automatic and predictable as Pavlov's dog salivating when he rang the bell[3]. The problem is exacerbated by the fact that the pastors and teachers who teach this are usually godly and righteous people whose teaching is otherwise correct and solid. Their disciples tend to "swallow whole" their teachings in total, thus making them unaware of subtle but significant errors within their teachings. It is much like the fish swallowing the "good worm" not realizing the unseen hook buried within. This phenomenon is alive and persistent within congregations, Bible schools, and Seminaries to this day.

This problem of swallowing error while feeding on otherwise "good food" works retroactively to the pastors and teachers themselves. They frequently spent many years studying from godly teachers to prepare for their ministries. Their teachers also were products of whole departments of "systematic theology" and the traditions of men. Thus, errors have a tendency to become "accepted theology" and fossilized in the minds of men. It was no different for the Pharisees in Mark 7. It is no different for theologians and Bible teachers today.

To seek a resolution to the questions regarding Torah observance for believers in Messiah, I have decided to bypass the usual ivory towers of academia with their theologians who are so skilled at weaving elaborate and lofty, erudite syllogisms, the many axioms of philosophical speculation and the varied postulations that emanate from the advanced mind of man. Instead,

I have decided to go to the ultimate source, the Author and Finisher of our faith, the Messiah, Himself.

What does the Messiah have to say about the place of the Torah (law) in the life of the believer? That would be a good place to start. In Matthew 5:17-19 Yeshua says "Don't think that I came to destroy the Torah or the Prophets. I didn't come to destroy but to fulfill. For most certainly, I tell you, until heaven and earth pass away, not even one smallest letter or one tiny pen stroke shall in any way pass away from the Torah until all things are accomplished. Therefore, whoever shall break one of these least commandments and teach others to do so, shall be called least in the Kingdom of Heaven; but whoever shall do and teach them shall be called great in the Kingdom of Heaven." This important and enlightening passage of Scripture provides many answers to the questions regarding the continuing validity and place of the Torah in the lives of believers.

Firstly, Yeshua boldly and emphatically declares His position on the Torah. He states that He did NOT come "to destroy the Torah or the Prophets". The word "destroy" means just that, to "abolish, overthrow or render inoperative".

He further states that He came to "fulfill". However you attempt to interpret the word "fulfill", Yeshua said it does NOT mean to "abolish, overthrow or render inoperative".

The words "abolish" and "fulfill" are common rabbinic terms historically used to describe interpretations of the Torah given during argumentation over the meaning of a passage. If a rabbi gave an incorrect interpretation, it was said that he "abolished the Torah". If he gave the correct interpretation, the rabbi would be said to have "fulfilled" the Torah, meaning he gave the Torah its proper, intended meaning.

Yeshua was saying that His intent with the Torah was NOT to give the wrong interpretation but to give the correct one. In no way should His words be misconstrued into saying He intended to "do away with" the Torah or make it inoperable. That, by the way, would disqualify Him from being the Messiah!

Secondly, Yeshua's positive view regarding the continuing authority and relevance of the Torah is further clarified in His saying "Until heaven and earth pass away, not even one smallest letter or one tiny pen stroke shall in any way pass away from the Torah until all things are accomplished." That sounds like a pretty permanent position on the subject. Since heaven and earth are still here and "all things" have yet to be fully accomplished, we can accept the rest of His statement regarding that even the smallest letter or tiny pen stroke in the Torah still has force and relevance.

Thirdly, His next statement adds more clarity. He states, "Therefore, whoever shall break one of these least commandments and teach others to do so, shall be called least in the Kingdom of Heaven; but whoever shall do and teach them shall be called great in the Kingdom of Heaven." The first observation to be made is that Yeshua is describing two different types of disciples, both of whom are "in the Kingdom of Heaven". One disciple not only breaks the commandments but also teaches others to do so as well. This may be likened to the current believer, pastor, or teacher who disregards the commandments and teaches others to also disregard them, thus "destroying" the Torah. This disciple's position in the kingdom is called "least". The other disciple Yeshua describes is one who not only does the commandments but also teaches others to do them as well. This may be likened to a current believer, pastor, or teacher who correctly does the commandments and teaches others to also do them, thus "fulfilling" the Torah. This disciple's position in the kingdom is called "great".

Of particular importance to note is that both disciples are "in" the kingdom. Torah observance is never about gaining a right standing with God or getting "in" to the Kingdom. Torah observance is never about earning or meriting salvation. It is never about legalism. That is the treadmill of works-righteousness that Paul wrote so strongly against. Instead, what this passage teaches is that Torah observance is the way of life for the believer and the fruit of that life will be manifested in those he or she teaches as they also embrace the Torah as the lifestyle of the redeemed.

So what about those passages by the Apostle Paul[4] that seem to contradict the above conclusions by the Messiah? The first response to this question is to assure the reader that there is no disagreement between Yeshua and Paul. Period. The harmony of the Scriptures is intact. Paul, himself, said in 1 Corinthians 11:1 "Be imitators of me, even as I also am of Messiah." If we ever think Paul is teaching something that is different from or in opposition to what Messiah taught, we need to go back to school and rethink how we have misinterpreted the writings of Paul.

Unfortunately for some, the pride of man has prevented some pastors, teachers, and theologians from doing just that. They have forged ahead with their errant teachings, ignored the harmony of the Scriptures, and developed a host of fanciful theories to justify their heresy. Let us not follow their example, but rather be faithful students of the Word of God.

Let us follow the example of the faithful Bereans in Acts 17:11 "Now these were more noble than those in Thessalonica, in that they received the word with all readiness of mind, examining the Scriptures daily to see whether these things were so." The Bereans were commended for receiving the word from Paul "with all readiness of mind" meaning they were teachable but also that they were committed to "examining the Scriptures daily to see whether these things were so."

What were the Scriptures they used as their authority to examine the teachings of Paul but the Tanach, referred to as the Old Testament, including the Torah? If Paul had deviated from the authority of the Torah, his teachings would have been and should have been rejected. It's the same today. That leaves no room for "the New Paul", "Paul seen in the New Light", "Paul as the Inventor of Christianity" or the Paul that taught "Bondage to the Law ended when Christ made all men free".

Let's examine a few Pauline Scriptures "with all readiness of mind" and "examine the Scriptures" like the Bereans. Paul's own example of Torah observance is instructive to use.

Acts 18:18 states "Paul, having stayed after this many more days, took his leave of the brothers, and sailed from there for Syria, together with Priscilla and Aquila. He shaved his head in Cenchreae, **for he had a vow**." This no doubt refers to the Nazarite vow described in Numbers 6:5 "All the days of his vow of separation no razor shall come on his head, until the days are fulfilled in which he separates himself to the LORD. He shall be holy. He shall let the locks of the hair of his head grow long." This was the vow that Paul intended to fulfill as described in Acts 21.

In Ephesians 6:2,3 we see Paul affirming the fifth commandment "Honor your father and mother," which is the first commandment with a promise: "that it may be well with you, and
you may live long on the earth."

In 1 Corinthians 9:8-10 Paul bases his argument regarding
support for ministers on the very Torah of Moshe, "Do I speak
these things according to the ways of men? Or doesn't the Torah
also say the same thing? For it is written in the Torah of Moses,
"You shall not muzzle an ox while it treads out the grain." Is it for
the oxen that God cares, or does he say it assuredly for our sake?
Yes, it was written for our sake, because he who plows ought to
plow in hope, and he who threshes in hope should partake of his
hope." Paul claims the authority and applicability of the Torah
of Moshe to the people and issues of his day. We would do well
to follow suit.

In Acts 21, we see the Apostle Paul giving a ministry report
to the Jerusalem Assembly with Ya'akov[5] and all the elders present. The brothers praised God for the wonderful report Paul
had given recounting all the fruit of his ministry among the
gentiles. The leadership then informed Paul about the believing
Jews there in Judea. In Acts 21:10 "They said to him, "You see,
brother, how many **thousands** there are among the Judeans
of those **who have believed**, and they are **all zealous for the
Torah**." The actual Greek word translated as thousands is the

word "myriad". A single myriad is ten thousand. Two myriads would be twenty thousand. Many myriads, as the text states, would be at least three or more which would calculate to a minimum of thirty thousand, possibly more as the phrase "how many myriads" doesn't have an upper limit! These large numbers of Jews in Judea are further described as those "who have believed" in the Messiah. Furthermore, it describes this large number of Messianic Jews as "all zealous for the Torah". There is no indication in the text that Ya'akov and the other elders or Paul had any issue with these large numbers of Messianic Jews being Torah-observant. Had they held the anti-Torah theology so common today, then their actions would have been quite different. Instead, we see them affirming their faithfulness to the Torah.

The Jerusalem leaders went on to say that these believers had been told that Paul had been teaching all the Jews to apostatize from Moshe, not to circumcise their sons, and not to follow the traditions. If Paul had been such an anti-Torah zealot, as is claimed today, he would have agreed with what was said about him and would have said, "At least they got that right!" Upon hearing the news of these tens of thousands of Jewish believers in Yeshua being "all zealous for the Torah" he would have set his hair on fire and screamed that they needed to be stopped, that they were all wrong and needed correction.

Instead, what did Paul do? His subsequent action of what he actually did destroys the popular argument of Paul being anti-Torah. He knew, as did the Jerusalem leaders, that these charges against him were **false**. They were false charges. Let that sink in. He proved his faithfulness to the Torah by agreeing to the wisdom of the Jerusalem leaders by agreeing to go to the temple to offer the appropriate Torah-prescribed sacrifices to complete his Nazarite vow and to also pay for the expenses for four others under the same vow.

The point of doing this was to demonstrate his Torah faithfulness in a very public way so that, according to Acts 21:24 "Then **all will know** that there is **no truth** in the things that they have been informed about you, but that **you yourself also walk keeping the Torah.**" This action by Paul, as created by and approved by the Jerusalem leaders, should resonate throughout the ages as a definitive statement demonstrating Paul's position regarding Torah observance in the life of the believer.

There remains, however, an issue with Paul with respect to Torah observance. There are a host of Scriptures that, on the surface, appear to either downplay or even negate Torah observance.

- Romans 3:28 states, "We maintain therefore that a man

is justified by faith apart from the works of the law."

- Romans 6:14 states, "For sin will not have dominion over you, for you are not under law, but under grace."

- Romans 7:4 states, "Therefore, my brothers, you also were made dead to the law through the body of Messiah"

- Romans 7:6 states, "But now we have been discharged from the law"

- Galatians 2:16 states, "knowing that a man is not justified by the works of the law"

- Ephesians 2:15 states, "having abolished in his flesh the hostility, the law of commandments contained in ordinances"

Wow, that's only a partial list of the many Scriptures where Paul is viewed as being anti-Torah.

Now the waters get real muddy . . .

On the other hand, there are many New Covenant Scriptures that offer a very Torah-positive view.

- John 14:15 states, "If you love me, keep my commandments."

- John 15:10 states, "If you keep my commandments, you will remain in my love."

- Romans 3:31 states, "Do we then nullify the law through faith? May it never be! No, we establish the law."

- Romans 7:12 states, "Therefore the law indeed is holy, and the commandment holy, righteous, and good."

- Romans 7:14 states, "For we know that the law is spiritual"

- Romans 7:16 states, "I consent to the law that it is good."

- Romans 7:22 states, "For I delight in God's Torah after the inward person."

- I Corinthians 7:19 states, "Circumcision[6] is nothing, and uncircumcision[7] is nothing, but what matters is keeping God's commandments."

Wow, that is also quite a list of Scriptures. What are we to make of this apparent conflict within the Word of God? Is the Bible unreliable? Does it contain errors? Is it a broken compass incapable of showing us the true North? Was the Apostle Paul confused or was he just pandering to the crowd? The answer, as always, is found in one word . . . context.

Those verses that, on the surface, appear to be anti-Torah are not so at all when properly examined in context.

Romans 3:28 and Galatians 2:16 correctly affirm that justification, that is, right standing before God, is by grace and not by works of law. This stands as a rebuke to a legalistic treadmill of works-righteousness to attain and keep one's standing before God.

Romans 6:14 can be best understood by looking at the word "under". It is true that we, as believers, are no longer "under" the condemnation of the Torah. Messianic author David Stern sees this verse as referring to "legalism" and I believe he is correct. If we are in the grace of God we are no longer "under" the bondage to legalism that characterized our previous relationship to God's Torah.

Romans 6:14, 7:4, 7:6, and Ephesians 2:15 all echo Paul's solid teaching against misuse of the Torah by perverting it into a legalistic, works-righteousness document.

Another important point to remember when attempting to understand Paul's writings is that his epistles or letters were written as responses to issues brought to his attention to address. Unfortunately, we do not have the questions, only Paul's responsive answers, which sometimes do inform as to the issue, but not always.

If we miss the issue, we will probably go down a false path in interpreting the writings of Paul.

When I studied law, I learned the standard formula used when briefing legal cases. It is called I.R.A.C. which stands for Issue, Rule, Application, and Conclusion. The Issue is of prime importance. If you get the issue wrong, then, even if you cite all manners of rules and find all manners of relevant applications, your conclusion may sound thoroughly logical and internally consistent but will be completely wrong.

I share this to remind us of the need to seek understanding regarding the various issues Paul was addressing in his writings. It is critical to realize that when Paul is speaking about the misuse of the Torah as a legalistic document as a means of obtaining salvation, it is understandable that he would present a rather harsh rebuke of such error. When he is speaking of the Torah as the God-inspired teaching for the lifestyle of the redeemed, which it is, Paul's words come across as very Torah-positive. It all depends on the context, doesn't it?

1. Chumash is related to the word "chamesh" which is Hebrew for the number five

2. From the Greek for "seventy" referring to the seventy Hebrew scholars who did the translation of the Torah into Greek around 250 BCE. It is sometimes written as LXX.

3. This was a famous experiment known as "Classical Conditioning" where Ivan Pavlov demonstrated that if you expose a dog to a bell tone every time he was fed, eventually he would involuntarily salivate in anticipation of eating even when the bell was sounded without providing food.

4. For a thorough and in-depth scholarly work on the Apostle Paul I highly recommend the book titled "The Letter Writer" by Tim Hegg available at www.torahresource.com and Amazon.

5. The name of the leader of the Jerusalem assembly and the brother of Yeshua should be rendered Ya'akov, certainly not James as is commonly done.

6. Saying circumcision was shorthand for saying "being Jewish".

7. Saying uncircumcision was shorthand for saying "being gentile".

Chapter Twenty-Four

God's Appointed Festivals

Who doesn't like a holiday? Time off from work! A family getaway! A road trip to Grandma's and Grandpa's! Celebrations with friends! Presents!

All of our major holidays[1] are so important to us that they are printed on our calendars and reminders pop up on our phones. It is good to have time set aside to pause and reflect and to be thankful for various people and events in our lives. We take time to celebrate our parents, our veterans, the founding of our nation, past U.S. Presidents, and the beginning of the New Year, at least according to the Gregorian calendar.

Among all the various holidays we celebrate, however, some have been forgotten. What about God's appointed times? In Leviticus 23:1,2 we learn about God's Appointment Calendar: "The LORD spoke to Moses, saying, "Speak to the children of Israel, and tell them, 'The **set feasts**[2] **of the LORD**, which you shall proclaim to be holy convocations, even these are **my set feasts**." Imagine that? God has a calendar too!

Some people see this chapter in Leviticus and their reaction is immediate. They say, "That was then" and "this is now". They say, "Those are for the Jews, not the Christians."

Let's take another look at the actual text. God Himself, says that these appointed times, these feasts are "the set feasts of the Lord" and "My set feasts". They are God's holidays. He meant them to be regular appointments where He would meet with His people in a special way. It is a promise He never rescinded.

Shabbat

The list of feasts in Leviticus 23 begins with the weekly Shabbat. Perhaps its placement at the beginning of the list and the fact that it is celebrated every week argues for its high importance to God. This day of rest and restoration is to be celebrated on the seventh day per God's Own design and purpose. He tells us that this special day is a **memorial of creation** in Exodus 20:11, "for in six days the LORD made heaven and earth, the sea, and all that is in them, and rested the seventh day; therefore the LORD blessed the Sabbath day, and made it holy." He also informs us in Deuteronomy 5:15 that Shabbat is a **memorial of redemption**, "You shall remember that you were a servant in the land of Egypt, and the LORD your God brought you out of there by a mighty hand and by an outstretched arm.

Therefore the LORD your God commanded you to keep the Sabbath day."

As believers in Messiah who have been granted "rest" in Him, can we not also embrace the weekly day that God set apart as holy, to recognize that "rest" that we have in Him and to celebrate the great deliverance He did in our lives? Is there a more appropriate day on which to do this than the day God set apart for this very purpose way back in Genesis 2? This is the special day included in the Ten Commandments. This day becomes especially important as we look to the future of His return and the establishment of His rule and reign on earth, which includes the weekly celebration of Shabbat as foreseen in Isaiah 56. Reason would argue that if we celebrated Shabbat "then" and we will celebrate Shabbat "later" as outlined in prophecy, then by what rationale do we suspend our celebration of Shabbat "now"?

Passover

Pesach or Passover is the next celebration on the list. It is a one-day festival that many people are familiar with. It is tied into the next festival called Chag HaMatzah or the feast of unleavened bread, which begins on the day of Passover and lasts a full week. This is where the term Passover week comes from. Passover is an annual festival in the spring of the year.[3]

It recounts God's gracious acts of mercy and strength in redeeming and rescuing the children of Israel from their bondage to Pharoah in Egypt. Who said there is no "grace" in the Old Testament? Everything about God's actions on behalf of His people is predicated on His grace! How could an oppressed people, literally "stuck in the mud", rise up against the all-powerful army of Pharoah and deliver themselves? No, it was God who declared in Exodus 6:6-8, "Therefore tell the children of Israel, 'I am the LORD, and I will bring you out from under the burdens of the Egyptians, and I will rid you out of their bondage, and I will redeem you with an outstretched arm, and with great judgments. I will take you to myself for a people. I will be your God; and you shall know that I am the LORD your God, who brings you out from under the burdens of the Egyptians. I will bring you into the land which I swore to give to Abraham, to Isaac, and to Jacob; and I will give it to you for a heritage: I am t he LORD.' "

Every year at the Passover seder[4] we celebrate the historical acts of our gracious Redeemer and Deliverer. It is a wonderful time to enjoy with our family and friends. This celebration, however, is not restricted to the remembrance of the historical exodus from Egypt.

- In the eating of the bitter herbs, we are reminded of the bitterness of our own past bondage to "Pharoah".

- In the types and shadows, we also see the picture of Messiah's great acts on our behalf.

- In the blood of the Passover lamb that was used to mark the homes of the Israelites thus saving them from death we see the blood of Messiah saving us from the death penalty prescribed for sin.

- In the "Last Supper," we see the elements in their fullest Messianic meaning.

- As Israel experienced redemption and deliverance from enslavement to their harsh taskmasters, so have we as believers in Messiah, through His blood.

- As Israel was challenged in Exodus 7:16, "Let my people go, **that they may serve me**" we learn that God's purpose in the redemption and deliverance of Israel was that of being set apart or sanctified. God did not redeem and deliver them to then set them free to do "whatever" in terms of their future.

- Their calling "out of" darkness was "into" the light of His Kingdom and His purposes for them.

Are we any different? The way some Evangelicals distort the gospel message into a quick fix, fire insurance, get-out-of-jail-free proposal ignores the purpose for which He saves us. The freedom for which we are saved exists only within the parameters God has designed for us to live within.

First Fruits

The next festival in Leviticus 23 is called "First Fruits". It is the annual celebration of the beginning of the barley harvest. The idea is to offer to God the "first" of our harvest to recognize His hand in the blessing of the fields. In so doing, we are thanking God for His provisions for us. What is more important to sustaining life than food?

Since most of us are not farmers and even those who are do not grow a lot of barley, does this festival have any meaning for us today? Does this have anything to do with Messiah? Absolutely!

In 1 Corinthians 15:20-22, it states, "But now Messiah has been raised from the dead. He became the **first fruit** of those who are asleep. For since death came by man, the resurrection of the dead also came by man. For as in Adam all die, so also in Messiah all will be made alive." Messiah rose from the dead on the day of the celebration of "First Fruits" picturing this meaning, that He would be the first of a much greater crop. What a reason to celebrate the feast of First Fruits as we see the intended picture of Messiah and the future ingathering of His people.

The Counting of the Omer[5]

After the festival of First Fruits, the Israelites are told to do a curious thing in Leviticus 23:15,16, "You shall count from the next day after the Sabbath, from the day that you brought the sheaf of the wave offering: **seven Sabbaths** shall be completed. The next day after the seventh Sabbath you shall count **fifty days**; and you shall offer a new meal offering to the LORD." Seven Sabbaths refers to seven weeks so seven times seven is forty nine with the next day being the fiftieth. This was the annual celebration of the harvest of wheat which is always a later crop than the barley. Once again, the idea is to present an offering from this crop to thank God for His provisions.

This festival is known as Shavuot, which is a Hebrew word meaning "weeks" and is based on the counting of the seven weeks. In Christian circles, it is more commonly known as Pentecost from the Greek for fifty, "pentekostos". The interesting question I often ask believers is this, "If Pentecost refers to fifty and the counting of fifty days, then what is the start date of the counting?" The answer I most often hear, other than "I don't know", is, "We count fifty days from Easter!" That answer could not be more incorrect.

I will address the origins of the word Easter and its celebrations in the next chapter. The main point right now is to recognize how this "tradition of men" regarding counting has deviated from what the text in Leviticus 23 actually states. The text is clear that the counting is to begin after the festival Shabbat on the feast of the First Fruits of the barley harvest. By changing the counting date to the idea of Easter, theologians have again revealed their bias. Church leaders did not want to establish a link between past festivals associated with Israel, so they renamed and redefined them. Indeed, the King James version of the Bible knowingly and intentionally inserts the word Easter in the text of Acts 12:4 in purposeful disregard of the Greek word "paschal" which should be translated as Passover. Modern translations have reversed this error. Instead of using the term Feast of Weeks, referring to this counting period from First Fruits, they use the term Pentecost. Instead of counting from the Shabbat of First Fruits, they decided to count from Easter. In doing all this, the impression is given that this Pentecost, as it is called, is something new and detached from Israel. This is true to such an extent that Pentecost is frequently and erroneously referred to as "the birthday of the Church" as a new entity. This concept is birthed directly from the previously addressed Replacement Theology and Dispensational models and represents two major errors infecting the body of Messiah today.

As God pours out His Spirit on the Jewish believers in Acts 2, they are divinely empowered to fulfill the missionary activity Yeshua had previously told them about in Luke 24:44-49, "He said to them, "This is what I told you while I was still with you, that all things which are written in the Torah of Moses, the Prophets, and the Psalms concerning me must be fulfilled." Then he opened their minds, that they might understand the Scriptures. He said to them, "Thus it is written, and thus it was necessary for the Messiah to suffer and to rise from the dead the third day, and that repentance and remission of sins should be preached in his name to all the nations, beginning at Jerusalem. You are witnesses of these things. Behold, I send out **the promise of my Father** on you. **But wait in the city of Jerusalem until you are clothed with power from on high.**"

Yom Teruah — the Feast of Trumpets

The next festival on the list of Leviticus 23 is the Feast of Trumpets. It is described as "a memorial of blowing of shofars[6]". It is also called Yom Teruah, the day of the blowing. If you have ever heard a shofar blown, you will never forget it. It is very loud and distinct. In most traditional Jewish and Messianic congregations, the day is marked by hearing the shofar blown over 100 times. There are various sounds that are made, done in a specific sequence, that add to the uniqueness of the day. So, what is all this blowing of the shofars supposed to accomplish? Historically, the shofar was heard at the giving of the Torah to Moshe. Since the sounds are loud and carried a long distance it is also easy to see how it was used to communicate during times of war, thus the different types of sounds used such as short, long, short then long, etc., had different meanings to better communicate tactical commands on a noisy battlefield.

Psalm 47:5 tells us of the joy of being in the presence of the King as it states, "God has gone up with a shout, the LORD with the sound of a **shofar**."

In Matthew 24:30,31 we see the shofar announcing the return of Messiah, "And then the sign of the Son of Man will appear in the sky. Then all the tribes of the earth will mourn, and they will see the Son of Man coming on the clouds of the sky with power and great glory. He will send out his angels with **a great sound of a shofar**, and they will gather together his chosen ones from the four winds, from one end of the sky to the other."

Also, 1 Thessalonians 4:16 states, "For the Lord himself will descend from heaven with a shout, with the voice of the archangel and with God's **shofar**." I long to hear THAT shofar!

It is stated in the text of Leviticus 23 that the next festival Yom Kippur is ten days after the blowing of the shofar. These intervening days between the two festivals are known in Judaism as the "days of awe". It is during this time that observant Jews are called to repentance, to turn to or return to Adonai and His Torah.

It is as if blowing the shofar is God's "wake-up call" to repentance. Does this have any relevance to people today? In a general sense, do you think people have gone off course and away from God and His Word? Do you think people "need" some kind of "wake-up call" to get their attention? You be the judge.

Yom Kippur

The next festival is Yom Kippur, which translates as the day of atonement. It is the annual day of repentance and renewal for all Israel. Prayer, fasting, and intercession play a large role with the most significant role played by the High Priest who offers prayers and sacrifices and enters the actual Holy of Holies only once a year. It is impossible to review all the teachings of Yom Kippur in this book but it is important to see how it is related to believers in Yeshua. All of the details of Yom Kippur point to Messiah's once-for-all sacrifice and His blood being the atonement for our souls. The crucified Messiah fulfills the picture of the mercy seat. It was His blood that He brought to the altar in Heaven. Each year we celebrate this festival, we can focus on Yeshua being God's only atonement and the great cost involved in securing our redemption. We learn that freedom is not free, it cost Yeshua His life. It cost the Father the pain of seeing His Son pay that price. We can also rejoice in the accomplished finished work of Messiah on our behalf. We can know with certainty that our names are written in the Lamb's Book of Life. What better way to focus on the primacy and centrality of Yeshua?

Sukkot or the Feast of Tabernacles

The last festival listed in Leviticus 23 is Sukkot, from the Hebrew meaning "booths" or "shelters". The Israelites were to construct these temporary structures and actually live in them for a week as a time of rejoicing. In Messianic congregations I have attended and been a part of it is indeed a time of rejoicing! It is designed by God to cause people to reflect and remember God as their provider during tough times. When Israel was in the desert, all they had was God. They had to depend on Him. Do we need a specific time to reflect on our own wilderness history and to remember God's covenant faithfulness to us as well? I believe we do. If we can recall His times of provision during the lean times, if we can recall His many blessings and guidance given, even when we were disobedient, how much more can we walk forward in faith believing what Yeshua said in Hebrews 13:5,6, "I will in no way leave you, neither will I in any way forsake you." So that with good courage we say, "The Lord is my helper. I will not fear. What can man do to me?" Yeshua also said in Matthew 28:20, "Behold, I am with you always, even to the end of the age."

---

1. The popular holidays known as Christmas and Easter will be commented on in the next chapter of the book.

2. The Hebrew word behind the translation of the word feasts is "moedim". In the singular form it is "moed".

3. Understanding and reconciling the Hebrew calendar system with our modern Gregorian system is no easy task. It is a complicated study. I recommend a book titled Judaism in a Nutshell: The Jewish Calendar by See-El Flores available at Amazon.

4. The Hebrew word "seder" means "order". There is a set order to the celebration which involves specific teachings and ceremonies.

5. The Hebrew word "omer" is a unit of measure of dry capacity used for counting.

6. A shofar is not technically a trumpet but a ram's horn.

Chapter Twenty-Five

Man's Festivals linked to paganism

S o far in our survey of the "traditions of men", we have observed the repeated pattern of man, in his state of rebellion, rejecting the authority and wisdom of the Word of God in favor of his own theories and inventions. It is foolish enough to seek ultimate truth from one's own mind, a questionable source of truth to begin with, but many of the "traditions of men" so commonplace in today's world also have their origin in "spiritually dark places". I am referring to the various manifestations of paganism that all have their ultimate origin in the demonic realm. They smell like smoke.

The problem of paganism is not new, although the term, itself, is thought to have originated during the Christian era and was used in a pejorative fashion. Originally, people associated with pagan beliefs did not normally call themselves "Pagans". Some groups today, however, proudly attach the name to themselves as Pagans or Neo-Pagans.

Names or titles aside, the issue of false religions that stand opposed to truth from God through His Word, has existed for a very long time. When we consider the very beginnings of rebellion with Adam and Eve, we see the picture of the serpent and his deceptions. He questioned the authority of the Word of God by asking in Genesis 3:1, "Has God really said?" Eve compounded the error by adding to the Word of God in Genesis 3:3, "You shall not touch it". The serpent then defied the written Word in Genesis 3:4, "You won't really die".

The lesson is clearly established that questioning, adding to, and defying the written Word of God introduces error. In the unfolding drama recorded for us in Genesis, the infection of rebellion did not take long to spread. By the time of Noach (Noah), it rose to such a level that God said the following in Genesis 6:5,6, "The LORD saw that the wickedness of man was great in the earth, and that every imagination of the thoughts of man's heart was continually only evil. The LORD was sorry that he had made man on the earth, and it grieved him in his heart."

Fast forward to the time of Genesis 11 which records the rebellious construction of the tower of Babel, which many scholars believe to have been an astrological tower devoted to the "gods of the heavens". Many of the perverse pagan ideas and practices that have spread throughout the world and have even infected current beliefs and practices within Christianity have their origin in Nimrod and Babylon[1].

By the time of Abraham, the concept of syncretism was firmly established. Syncretism is the combining of the holy and the profane, truth, and error, the embracing of false teachings and mixing it with the true. Joshua commented in Joshua 24:2, "Joshua said to all the people, "The LORD, the God of Israel, says, 'Your fathers lived of old time beyond the River, even Terah, the father of Abraham, and the father of Nahor. **They served other gods.**" This was the world in which Abraham grew up. This was the world that God called him out of. God physically separated Abraham and his family from the corrupting influences of all the other people surrounding him. Through Isaac and Jacob, God continued His protective shepherding care of His people by guarding them from the surrounding influences of false religions.

In giving the Torah to His covenant people through the hand of Moshe, God was establishing His teachings as the standard and norm. Within the Torah itself are contained several teachings that are curious to the modern observer. The Israelites were not to mix things that were essentially different, such as crops, wool, linen, etc. Modern man looks at these and sees them as ridiculous, so he ignores them. What if God was using these commandments to teach the Israelites an important principle?

Every time they obeyed this and saw others obeying it, they were reminded of the prohibitions regarding mixing things that don't belong together. Do you see the idea here? God is protecting His people from the idea of syncretism. The fact is, He hates it.

Deuteronomy 6:4,5 states, "Hear, Israel: the LORD is our God. The LORD is one. You shall love the LORD your God with all your heart, with all your soul, and with all your might." No room here for divided loyalties. Yeshua affirms this in Matthew 22:37,38, "Yeshua said to him, " 'You shall love the Lord your God with all your heart, with all your soul, and with all your mind.' This is the first and great commandment." Perfect continuity of thought here, as we would expect.

During the checkered history of Israel, we see the familiar pattern of man's rebellious nature and his propensity to willingly embrace traditions and practices that clearly come from pagan sources. We see the constant references to the "high places" that were rarely taken down, even during the reign of otherwise godly kings. These high places were shrines of worship to a pantheon of false gods. The surrounding Moabites and Canaanites had indeed become a source of spiritual degradation to the people of Israel.

The problem was made worse by the failure of the priesthood who had become corrupt and not faithful to their calling as described in Ezekiel 44:23, "They shall teach my people the difference between the holy and the common, and cause them to discern between the unclean and the clean." This construct of identification and separation is a clear reference to the avoidance of syncretism, which is its polar opposite. The priests clearly failed in their duties here.

It is the same with us. Many of us "grew up" in a religious world that has embraced much error. Our "traditions of men" frequently include practices that have their origin in paganism. Like the corrupted priests in ancient Israel, our spiritual leaders have also failed "to teach my people the difference between the holy and the common and cause them to discern between the unclean and the clean." This is partly due to the theological bias that reduces or eliminates the authority of the Torah in the life of today's believers. It also stems from a different issue, that of the "social gospel" that has its basis in being "seeker-friendly" and only "positive", which gets redefined to mean "don't say anything that might offend someone."

One time, after a sermon I gave that was pretty hard-hitting, a person asked me, "Don't you think that might have hurt someone's pride?" My response was, "Hurt it? I was trying to kill it outright!"

The problem of syncretism is that it seeks to be friends with the world at the expense of God's truth. It panders to the fleshly nature with its promises of worldly success and riches. Remember the devil tempting Messiah in Matthew 4:8-10, "Again, the devil took him to an exceedingly high mountain and showed him all the kingdoms of the world and their glory. He said to him, "I will give you all of these things if you will fall down and worship me." Then Yeshua said to him, "Get behind me, Satan! For it is written, 'You shall worship the Lord your God, and you shall serve him only.'"

Do we see the pull of the world today in the vain philosophies that seek to separate thought and practices from the Word of God? Like Abraham of old, God is also calling us out. 2 Corinthians 6:17 says, 'Come out from among them, and be separate,' says the Lord.

Christmas

Many scholarly works[2] have been written on the pagan sources of the practices surrounding the modern celebration of Christmas. I do not wish to reproduce all those arguments here. I do, however, want to challenge the reader a little by asking a few questions. These are provided for the reader to do their own research to establish the certainty of the origin of each practice and to further research what the Bible has to say about the subject.

- What is the winter solstice and how does that relate to

the date assigned to Christmas?

- Do you know the origin of the Yule log?

- What was the Saturnalia?

- Was the celebration of Christmas ever outlawed by the church?

- Who was "Saint Nicholas"?

- Where did the gift-giving come from?

- Where did the tradition of the evergreen tree come from?

- Does Jeremiah 10 speak of Christmas trees?

- What about reindeer, holly, and mistletoe?

- Have you ever wondered why the date of the birth of Yeshua is not recorded in Scripture?

- How is it that there is no historical record of believers celebrating the birth of the Messiah for several hundred years after the fact?

- Who was Constantine and what did he assert regarding the practices of the church?

I will leave the reader to the task of researching and differentiating between the holy and the common, between the unclean and the clean. May God guide you and reveal His truth to you. May you be blessed with the courage to follow His Word over the precepts of man.

Easter

Another holiday that needs to be addressed is that of Easter. It is important to note that the word "Easter", like the word "Christmas" and the word "church", is not a Bible word. None of these words are to be found within the pages of Scripture in Hebrew or Greek. Various translators like to fiddle with the text to insert them as the King James version does in Acts 12:4. Shame on them.

As previously mentioned, Yeshua was resurrected on the feast of First Fruits, which fits the prophetic significance of that particular feast. As already discussed, 1 Corinthians 15:20-22 demonstrates this interpretation.

In understanding the derivation of the name Easter, a little history is in order. There was a Babylonian goddess named Ishtar. In the land of Canaan, she was referred to as Astarte. Originally, she was celebrated as the goddess of Spring and was called Eostre, also known as Ostara, Austra, and Eastre. There are four cardinal points on the pagan calendar, the Solstices and the Equinoxes. The celebration of Ishtar was tied to the always-changing date of the Spring Equinox. Why? This was the day when the sun began shining longer making the day longer. It was seen as the light conquering over the darkness, the start of Spring. Is it not interesting that even today, per Church councils that began under Constantine in 325 CE, the annual date for Easter is still determined to be the first Sunday following the full moon after the vernal equinox, according to the Pagan calendar?

The emperor Constantine made many changes to the practices of the church. In his desire to make an easy pathway for the pagans, a "seeker-friendly" approach, he took existing pagan holidays and "baptized" them into the church. Thus, the pre-existing pagan celebration of the Saturnalia on or about December 25th became the chosen date to celebrate Christmas. The preexisting pagan holiday of the worship of the sun made Christian observance of Sunday official. The pre-existing pagan celebration tied to the celebration of the goddess of the Spring, Eastre or Ishtar, became tied by the pagan calendar to the date that became known as Easter.

Since the resurrection of Messiah happened on the feast of First Fruits and that was tied by the Biblical calendar to Passover which happens on the 14th of the month Nisan, according to the Jewish calendar, then why is Easter, allegedly a holiday to celebrate His resurrection, tied to a pagan holiday? This is because Easter is linked to the pagan concept of the birth of Spring and not the resurrection of the Messiah. Why else do we see the prevalence of pagan fertility symbols such as bunny rabbits and eggs, commonly associated with the celebration of Easter?

I can hear the objection already. "So, knowing the origin of the name "Easter" and its association with the pagan fertility goddess of the spring, what's the big deal? After all, we're only really celebrating the resurrection of the Messiah, right?" I do not say that Christians are knowingly celebrating a pagan goddess. I do question if they're celebrating the resurrection of the Messiah "under the name of another god". It may be done in ignorance, and I believe that to be mostly true, but now that you **do** know, what will you do about it?

Ephesians 5:10,11 states, "proving what is well pleasing to the Lord. Have no fellowship with the unfruitful deeds of darkness, but rather even reprove them."

Halloween

As I write these words, we are beginning the month of October which culminates in the well-known holiday of Halloween, also referred to as "All Hallow's Eve". The stores have already begun their marketing campaigns spanning several aisles. Everything from candy and costumes to party decorations and outside displays to transform your home into spooky images designed to frighten and entertain. It's the time of year to dress up our children, and even a few adults, in various costumes, usually depicting the horror, macabre spectres of the denizens of the deep, dark world of the scary afterlife. We see them looking like witches, demons, ghosts, vampires, zombies, mummies and various grotesque creatures. It is likened to "hell on earth". It is the time when we place the carved-out pumpkin[3], known as the jack-o-lantern, on the porch with its candle projecting various evil faces. It is the time when we send out our children to go door-to-door to engage in trick-or-treating, as it is called today.

Why has this weird holiday become so popular in our culture? What do we know of its history and meaning? Most importantly, what does the Bible say to us about engaging in these practices?

First, let's review a little history of the four cardinal points on the pagan calendar. The pagans divided their worship system into a highly organized, sequential division of time governed by the movement of the sun, moon, and stars. Various meanings were then assigned to these observations.

It is important to realize that while we know true science accords with the heliocentric fact that the Earth actually revolves around the sun, the historical descriptions given from the perspective of the observer on Earth make it appear that the sun is moving.

In the fall, the Autumnal Equinox was the celebration timed to coincide with when the Sun is exactly above the Equator causing the day and night to be of equal length. The days immediately begin to get shorter and the nights longer. This marks the beginning of the season known as fall which continues until the Winter Solstice. During this time, in the Northern Hemisphere, where we reside in the United States, the sun has the shortest path in the sky, making the shortest amount of daylight and making the night the longest of the year. The Vernal Equinox in the spring is when, once again, the sun is exactly above the Equator causing the day and night to be of equal length. The days immediately begin to be longer until the Summer Solstice, when the sun has the longest path in the sky of the Northern Hemisphere making the daylight the longest of the year.

Having described the actual processes and how they create the seasonal changes that we observe here on planet Earth, the pagans took these points on the calendar and assigned all manner of occultic meanings and associated practices to them. In fact, the origins of pagan practices go all the way back to ancient Babylon, the source of many modern pagan practices embraced by Christianity. Thus, the Romans embraced the feast of Saturnalia, from December 17 – 24, with much-associated drunkenness and orgies, etc. The 25th was seen as the "rebirth" of the sun so it was a cause to celebrate. It was later chosen by the emperor Constantine as a day to commemorate the birth of the Messiah. This was useful in that the pagans were already observing the day and no pressure was needed to establish a different day on their calendar. Talk about creating a "seeker-friendly" congregation!

The Vernal Equinox in the spring was seen as the rebirth of life itself and even of the gods that were worshipped, such as Tammuz and Damuzi. Thus, we have Maypoles, bunnies, and eggs, all symbols of fertility.

The Summer Solstice is known for celebrations of drunkenness and excess, known in Britain as Midsummer Night.

The Autumnal Equinox became associated with the dying and decaying of nature and with death itself. The ancient Celts revered this day as the start of the New Year, known by the name Samhain, pronounced: "sow-in". It predates Christianity by thousands of years. Of interest to our study, is that this particular point on the calendar coincides with the modern celebration of Halloween. It was taught that the separation between the worlds of the living and the dead was at its thinnest point during this time. It was at midnight that human sacrifices were offered to appease the spirit world.

The original colonists in America were rigidly opposed to anything connected to paganism and the celebrations were unknown until later. A surge in witchcraft and satanism spread in this country stemming from folk customs and pagan superstitions from immigrant Celtic and Druidic sources.

The pagan festival of Samhain has traditional colors of black and orange and utilizes fire as a frequent symbol. In fact, "bone fires" or "bonfires", known as "Samghnagans", were associated with protection from fairies and witches and were also used for cleansing rituals. The people would dress up in various costumes to trick evil spirits into not recognizing them. They would frequently go door-to-door requesting food and drink. They were given "soul cakes" as a reward for singing to the dead. The idea of trick-or-treating in costume was born from this practice.

So, what do we make of the current, popular practice within so much of Christianity that wants to embrace this holiday? How do we rationalize such blatantly pagan and occultic celebrations and meanings? Do we follow the error of the Roman Catholic church that sought to "baptize" paganism into the church by adopting and attempting to redefine the practices? We already have God's appointed festivals, which include several harvest festivals to rejoice for His provisions. An excellent example is the festival of Sukkot or the Feast of Tabernacles where we remember and rejoice in God's provisions for us. What do we say to the current trend of creating new **"Harvest Festivals"** for our children, complete with costumes and trick-or-treating, all of which, of course, is claimed to be done in "the Name of the Lord"? Is the modern church so bereft of meaningful celebrations that they need to borrow from the pagans? How far from the Bible have church leaders gone? In large measure, Christianity has lost its Scriptural compass!

There are several responses to all these practices from the Bible.

- Deuteronomy 18:9-14 states, "When you have come into the land which the LORD your God gives you, **you shall not learn to imitate the abominations of those nations**. There shall not be found with you anyone who makes his son or his daughter pass through the fire, one who uses divination, one who tells fortunes, or an enchanter, or a sorcerer, or a charmer, or someone who consults with a familiar spirit, or a wizard, or a necromancer. For whoever does these things is an abomination to the LORD. Because of these abominations, the LORD your God drives them out from before you. You shall be blameless with the LORD your God. For these nations that you shall dispossess listen to those who practice sorcery and to diviners; but as for you, the LORD your God has not allowed you so to do."

1. Pass through fire refers to child sacrifice to the pagan god Moloch.

2. Divination refers to foretelling the future through occult means.

3. Consulting with a familiar spirit was an element of witchcraft.

4. Wizardry refers to magical powers.

5. Fortune telling is connected to occultic sources.

6. An Enchanter or Charmer is one who influences others by magical charms and incantations.

7. Sorcery refers to power from evil spirits and/or drugs.

8. A Necromancer is one who conjures up the spirits of the dead for power.

- Deuteronomy 20:17,18 states, "But you shall utterly

destroy them: the Hittite, the Amorite, the Canaanite, the Perizzite, the Hivite, and the Jebusite, as the LORD your God has commanded you; **that they not teach you to follow all their abominations**, which they have done for their gods; so would you sin against the LORD your God."

- Leviticus 19:31 states, "Don't turn to those who are mediums, nor to the wizards. Don't seek them out, to be defiled by them. I am the LORD your God."

- Ephesians 4:27 states, "And don't give place to the devil."

- Ephesians 5:11 states," Have **no fellowship** with the unfruitful deeds of darkness, but rather even reprove them."

- 1 Corinthians 10:21 states, "You can't both drink the cup of the Lord and the cup of demons. You can't both partake of the table of the Lord and of the table of demons."

- 1 Peter 5:8 states, "Be sober and self-controlled. Be watchful. Your adversary, the devil, walks around like a roaring lion, seeking whom he may devour."

- 1 Thessalonians 5:22 states, "Abstain from every form of evil."

- Isaiah 5:20 states, "Woe to those who call evil good, and good evil; who put darkness for light, and light for darkness."

- Romans 13:12 states, "The night is far gone, and the day is near. Let's therefore throw off the deeds of darkness, and let's put on the armor of light."

- James 4:7 states, "Be subject therefore to God. Resist the devil, and he will flee from you."

- Ephesians 5:15,16 states, "Therefore watch carefully how you walk, not as unwise, but as wise, redeeming the time, because the days are evil."

- John 3:19,20 states, "This is the judgment, that the light has come into the world, and men loved the darkness rather than the light, for their works were evil. For everyone who does evil hates the light and doesn't come to the light, lest his works would be exposed."

- Galatians 4:8-10 states, "However at that time, not knowing God, you were in bondage to those who by nature are not gods. But now that you have come to know God, or rather to be known by God, why do you turn back again to the weak and miserable elemental principles, to which you desire to be in bondage all over again? You observe days, months, seasons, and years."

Given the pagan and occultic sources of the practices of Halloween, given their emphasis on the powers of darkness, given their connections to the spirit world, and given their witness of and attraction to these powers, I do not see any redeeming value or justification to ignore the clear teachings from the Word of God in embracing such obvious errors of satanic origin. They are from the pit of hell and they smell like smoke! I will follow the wise counsel of Joshua in Joshua 24:15 which states, ". . . but as for me and my house, we will serve the LORD."

---

1. See a book titled The Two Babylons by Alexander Hislop.

2. An excellent work is "Why I Don't Celebrate Christmas" by Tim Hegg available at www.torahresource.com. Also do a web search for The History Channel on The History of Christmas.

3. The original pagans in Britain used a carved turnip. In America, the tradition evolved into carving a pumpkin.

Chapter Twenty-Six

Holy Cow! What's on the Menu ?

There is a need to address the various "traditions" associated with what the Bible, specifically the Apostolic Writings or the New Testament, teaches about food. This section applies equally to Roman Catholic as well as Protestant traditions on the subject. It represents one of the traditions each camp basically has in common.

Before examining the various Scriptures that deal with the subject, I feel it necessary to restate a disclaimer. The decisions people make regarding what they believe the Bible says about food are not in any way linked to their individual status of salvation before God. I am not asserting any form of legalism here. If people read these comments and conclude differently and go ahead with their practice of eating pork and shellfish, their salvation status before God remains unchanged. They are not more or less "saved" than any other true believer in the Messiah. Although, from a purely health standpoint, I might suggest that eating pork and shellfish may not keep you from Heaven but it just might send you there sooner.

As previously demonstrated, the Bible has a baseline list in Leviticus 11 about what constitutes food and what does not. It is helpful to remember that when Israel received the Torah and agreed to the covenant, they were composed of native-born Jews as well as the "mixed multitude" of gentiles who left Egypt and were part of that same community. They all declared in Exodus 19:8, as one, "All the people answered together, and said, "All that the LORD has spoken we will do." There was one Torah for the native-born and the foreigners with them. Leviticus 24:22 states, "You shall have one kind of law for the foreigner as well as the native-born; for I am the LORD your God." Numbers 15:15,16 states, "For the assembly, there shall be one statute for you and for the stranger who lives as a foreigner, a statute forever throughout your generations. As you are, so the foreigner shall be before the LORD. One law and one ordinance shall be for you and for the stranger who lives as a foreigner with you.' "

There was never any room for two separate standards of teaching based on whether one was Jewish or gentile. There was, and remains, One Torah for all.

As we saw in previous chapters, gentiles have been "grafted in" to the remnant of believing Jews. According to Ephesians 2 and 3, they are now fellow citizens, fellow heirs, fellow members, and fellow partakers. They are no longer foreigners and strangers but members of the covenants embodying God's promise. The Torah, God's gracious instructions for the redeemed community, is for them as well.

We have already addressed some common traditions of men, such as Replacement Theology and Dispensationalism, that would attempt to separate believers from a significant portion of the Word of God. Let us look at some other traditions of interpretation that essentially attempt to do the same.

There are a number of "traditional" interpretations of select New Testament passages that seek to create a "new teaching" at variance with what the Bible explicitly establishes about food in Leviticus 11. That, in itself, should be a clue about any interpretive schema that changes the Word of God or makes it "flexible to the whims of man". It is either the absolute, unerring, inspired, and authoritative Word from God Himself that He claims is unchanging and eternal or it is merely the creation of the minds of men and, therefore, just one opinion among many on any matter. Let's examine these Scriptures one by one and see what they actually tell us.

Mark 7

We began this book with a careful and thorough examination of Mark 7 and learned that Yeshua was teaching that clean,

Biblical foods do not become unclean merely by the avoidance of the man-made ceremonial ritual hand-washing tradition of the Pharisees. That is the context of His declaring "all foods clean", although, as we saw, the insertion of that phrase into the text is not based on any early manuscripts. The passage in Mark 7 does not speak to the issues surrounding eating unclean meats.

Acts 10 – Peter's Pork Picnic

One of the most frequent passages that enters into conversations about food is Acts 10. I have heard people refer to this as God's revelation to Peter that He had made everything clean to eat and that Peter should reverse his previously held scruples and go ahead and have a ham sandwich. Could this possibly be true? If God can reverse His teaching on this, what would prevent Him from reversing any teaching, including our salvation status in Him? Theologians and Bible students need to be cautious of any teaching that has the net effect of altering the Word of God. Remember the issue between Eve and the serpent in the garden? The first command that mankind broke was a food law. Just sayin.

Remember how we previously learned the importance of defining the "issue" in seeking to understand any passage of Scripture? So what's the issue being dealt with in Acts 10?

The passage begins in Acts 10:1,2 stating, "Now there was a certain man in Caesarea, Cornelius by name, a centurion of what was called the Italian Regiment, a devout man, and **one who feared God** with all his house, who gave gifts for the needy generously to the people, and always prayed to God." Where the text describes Cornelius as "one who feared God" it is actually translating the Greek word "phoboumenoi" meaning "God-fearers". This term does not merely reflect a person's morality as such. It does not mean, "He is a God-fearing man." It was a legal and technical term for a specific type of gentile who was drawn to the worship of the God of Abraham but chose to not undergo formal ritual conversion[1] to "become a Jew", a practice, by the way, entirely man-made without any Scriptural foundation. These "God-fearers" were already conversant with the Torah and observant of its teachings, including the food laws of Leviticus 11. Quite possibly, the only reason Cornelius opted for this intermediate status of God-fearer instead of full ritual conversion was his military position. Certainly, the politics of his "converting" would have been an issue for him and his future with Rome. Without a doubt, any leader in the Roman army could not be perceived as having divided loyalties.

The text continues to show Cornelius being visited by an angel with an important message in Acts 10:3-8, "At about the ninth hour of the day, he clearly saw in a vision an angel of God coming to him and saying to him, "Cornelius!" He, fastening his eyes on him and being frightened, said, "What is it, Lord?" He said to him, "Your prayers and your gifts to the needy have gone up for a memorial before God. Now send men to Joppa, and get Simon, who is also called Peter. He is staying with a tanner named Simon, whose house is by the seaside. When the angel who spoke to him had departed, Cornelius called two of his household servants and a devout soldier of those who waited on him continually. Having explained everything to them, he sent them to Joppa."

It is significant that Cornelius was praying at the ninth hour of the day. According to the Jewish reckoning of time, this was at 3:00 in the afternoon, the time of the afternoon prayers at the Temple. As a gentile drawn to the worship of the God of Abraham, it was only natural for him to follow the same pattern.

Through this vision of an angel and his message to Cornelius, God set in motion the sending of men to the city of Joppa to seek out Simon Peter. I find it interesting that God was working behind the scenes and orchestrating events and situations to further His plan long before Peter had his vision.

Is this not true of us, as well? We are not aware of all that God is doing for us, outside our scope of understanding and vision. Our lack of awareness should never be misunderstood as proof of God's lack of care towards us. It has been said, "When you don't understand what the hand of God is doing, trust His heart."

In Acts 10:9-16 we see the story unfolding, "Now on the next day as they were on their journey and got close to the city, Peter went up on the housetop to pray at about noon. He became hungry and desired to eat, but while they were preparing, he fell into a trance. He saw heaven open and a certain container descending to him, like a great sheet let down by four corners on the earth, in which were all kinds of four-footed animals of the earth, wild animals, reptiles, and birds of the sky. A voice came to him, "Rise, Peter, kill and eat!" But Peter said, "Not so, Lord; for I have never eaten anything that is common or unclean." A voice came to him again the second time, "What God has cleansed, you must not call unclean." This was done three times, and immediately the thing was received up into heaven."

Unfortunately, some people stop reading at this point and force a conclusion to their inquiry. They assert, "Since God has cleansed all these animals and redesignated them as kosher to eat, then Peter was free to have a pulled pork sandwich." Not so fast.

First, remember that this was a "vision" that Peter had. It was not reality. He did not eat anything. This vision happened "while they were preparing" the meal.

Secondly, the meaning can be understood as a test of what standard Peter would use to respond to the challenge to "rise, kill, and eat." Peter's response demonstrates his fidelity to the Torah to define what is kosher food and what is not. He tells the Lord "for I have never eaten anything that is common or unclean." For Peter, the only source of definition of what is "common or unclean" was the Torah. His answer showed that he passed the test. Instead of the traditions of men, Peter's standard for determining what is acceptable to eat is found in the Torah. This becomes critical for Peter as God later reveals to him how his bias in rejecting gentiles is based on the traditions of men and not the Word of God.

Thirdly, we know that Peter did not suddenly believe that God had changed His mind on the food laws of Leviticus 11 because of the very next verses in Acts 10:17-20 which state, " Now while **Peter was very perplexed in himself what the vision which he had seen might mean**, behold, the men who were sent by Cornelius, having made inquiry for Simon's house, stood before the gate, and called and asked whether Simon, who was also called Peter, was lodging there. **While Peter was pondering the vision**, the Spirit said to him, "Behold, three men seek you. But arise, get down, and go with them, doubting nothing; for I have sent them."

After the vision had been played out three times, the text informs us that "Peter was **very perplexed in himself** what the vision which he had seen might mean". He still didn't get it.

Before we look down our noses at Peter's apparent denseness in not comprehending the meaning, we should consider how many times God has tried to communicate things to our own, oftentimes stubborn, minds. At any rate, it is clear that Peter did not interpret the vision as a green light for a bacon sandwich or a shrimp cocktail. Peter was still trying to comprehend what God was telling him through this vision. It was not immediately clear to him.

The text continues in Acts 10:21-23, "Peter went down to the men, and said, "Behold, I am he whom you seek. Why have you come?" They said, "Cornelius, a centurion, a righteous man and one who fears God, and well-spoken of by all the Jewish nation, was directed by a holy angel to invite you to his house, and to listen to what you say." So, he called them in and provided a place to stay." To Peter's credit, he obeyed the message in the vision, received the visitors as his overnight guests and the next day he and some brothers accompanied them to Joppa to visit Cornelius.

Now we come to the "Aha!" moment for Peter in Acts 10:23-28, "On the next day Peter arose and went out with them, and some of the brothers from Joppa accompanied him. On the next day, they entered into Caesarea. Cornelius was waiting for them, having called together his relatives and his near friends. When Peter entered, Cornelius met him, fell down at his feet, and worshiped him. But Peter raised him up, saying, "Stand up! I myself am also a man." As he talked with him, he went in and found many gathered together. He said to them, "You yourselves know how it is an **unlawful thing** for a man who is a Jew to join himself or come to one of another nation, but **God has shown me that I shouldn't call any man unholy or unclean**."

Peter's declaration that they "know" how it is an "unlawful thing" for a Jew to have interaction with a gentile betrays the source of that tradition of men. Nowhere in the Torah is such a "law" found. Israel was always destined to be a light to the gentiles. There is nothing about gentiles that needs to be avoided. The only separation involves pagan beliefs and practices, but never the people themselves. As previously mentioned in our study, there is nothing in the Torah about restricting a Jew from having fellowship with or entering the home of a gentile. Peter was struggling with the common prejudice of the day that arose from the man-made Eighteen Measures against contact with gentiles.

The significant statement by Peter that "God has shown me that I shouldn't call any **man** unholy or unclean" is a full and satisfying answer to the meaning of Peter's vision. Peter had passed the test regarding the food challenge by applying the correct standard, the Torah, instead of man-made traditions. Here God is asking Peter to follow suit in applying the same standard, the Torah, to the issue of acceptance of gentiles instead of the traditions of men he was previously in bondage to.

Later in Acts 10:34 Peter boldly declares, "Truly I perceive that **God doesn't show favoritism**; but in **every nation** he who fears him and works righteousness is acceptable to him." This was a radical departure for Peter as well as the others with him.

Peter began sharing the gospel with them. In Acts 10:44-48 it states, "While Peter **was still speaking these words**, the Holy Spirit fell on all those who heard the word. They of the circumcision who believed were amazed, as many as came with Peter, because the gift of the Holy Spirit **was also poured out on the Gentiles**. For they heard them speaking in other languages and magnifying God. Then Peter answered, "Can anyone forbid these people from being immersed with water? They have received the Holy Spirit **just like us**." He commanded them to be immersed in the name of Yeshua the Messiah."

The significance of the Holy Spirit's coming upon these gentiles "during" Peter's sermon demands comment. First, it demonstrates the sovereignty of the Holy Spirit. Second, it shows that these gentiles were filled with the Holy Spirit before they had any chance to submit to the false, man-made ritual that had misused circumcision as a conversion ritual that would allegedly "make them into Jews". This was proof positive that this was not a God-ordained requirement for gentiles. The text also says that these gentiles were saved "just like us". How are Jews saved? By grace through faith in the Messiah. How are gentiles saved? By grace through faith in the Messiah. Period. No other man-made rituals are necessary.

In Acts 11:2,3 we see the reaction of some legalistic brothers in Jerusalem, "When Peter had come up to Jerusalem, those who were of **the circumcision** contended with him, saying, "You went into uncircumcised men and ate with them!" Imagine their reaction when they learned that Peter actually went into the home and even ate with gentiles. Oh, the shock of it all. Do you see how deeply held traditions of men can hold even believers captive and in bondage to false teachings that run counter to the Word of God? Remember, these legalistic critics of Peter were also believers!

Peter retold his story about the vision and its meaning. The sequence of events proves the sovereignty of the Holy Spirit and refutes the traditions of men regarding the legalistic teachings of "the circumcision faction" within the congregation in Jerusalem. Peter demonstrated that he finally understood the clear meaning of the vision when he said, "God has shown me that I shouldn't call any **man** unholy or unclean". The vision had **nothing to do with food** or the abrogation of the Torah's teaching regarding food as listed in Leviticus 11. It was all about Peter's prejudice against gentiles based solely on man-made traditions.

1 Tim 4:1-5

The next text that comes up in discussions about food bears investigation. In Paul's first letter to his young disciple Timothy, he is sharing much wise counsel to help him in his ministry. Timothy is warned about people wanting to teach a "different doctrine", espousing "myths" and "vain talking". He is given instruction on qualifications for ministry. He is warned about "seducing spirits" and "doctrines of demons". He is told to turn away from "empty chatter and oppositions of what is falsely called knowledge". Wise words that apply to today as well. If these words had been heeded by ministers today, perhaps there would be no need for the book you are reading.

The text that frequently comes up in discussions about food is 1 Tim 4:1-5 which states, "But the Spirit says expressly that in later times some will fall away from the faith, paying attention to seducing spirits and doctrines of demons, through the hypocrisy of men who speak lies, branded in their own conscience as with a hot iron, **forbidding marriage** and **commanding to abstain from foods which God created to be received with thanksgiving** by those who believe and know the truth. For every creature of God is **good**, and **nothing is to be rejected** if it is received with thanksgiving. For it is **sanctified through the word of God** and prayer."

One of the main errors that Paul was writing against was the expanding menace of Gnosticism. It was growing in popularity among the intellectuals, even within believing communities. This theory sees all physical things as of a lower order and only places value on spiritual, ethereal qualities. This is in stark contrast to the fact that when God made the world and mankind He said it was good! The Gnostics were a cultic system that valued knowledge above all else. Indeed, the word Gnostic is from the Greek word "gnosis" referring to knowledge or insight. This had the effect of distorting the gospel message into something akin to a "New Age" redefinition of terms. These cultic teachers taught that the body was inferior and, thus, evil. They redefined salvation as knowledge of a hidden divinity within, as opposed to the true gospel message of repentance and the new birth. Gnostics also tended to be strict vegetarians and adopted a strict ascetic practice of celibacy and viewed marriage as less than spiritual in their definitions.

When we examine the text in light of this background, we see what issue Paul is responding to. He is rejecting the Gnostic teaching that "forbids marriage" and "commanding to abstain from foods which God created to be received with thanksgiving".

God is the author of marriage. In the book of Genesis, He designed it, defined it, and continues to bless it.

He also gave instructions regarding food in Leviticus 11. When the text in 1 Timothy states "foods which God created to be received", it can only refer back to where He lists and defines those foods that were "created to be received" and that is Leviticus 11. This is clear from Paul's statement that these were "sanctified through the word of God". Sanctified means set apart so where did God "set apart" these foods but Leviticus 11? God created "those foods" and defined them as "food to be received". He did not change His mind. Paul was condemning these false teachers who went beyond the Word of God to prohibit Biblically "clean" foods.

1 Corinthians 10:23-33

Paul is giving instructions to the believers who are living in one of the most pagan cities anywhere. In fact, the phrase "to play the Corinthian" refers to very loose moral behavior. Corinth was a city wholly given over to idolatry and all manner of licentiousness and sexual immorality. I can think of a few cities within our own country that are similar.

The challenge for the new, gentile believers living within this city was how to avoid idolatry, in all its forms. One of the problems was the meat markets. Meat that was sold in these markets was frequently offered in idol worship within the surrounding pagan temples prior to being sold in the markets. These new gentile believers were not sure whether eating such meat would be tantamount to participating in idolatry or if it was permitted.

The text states, "All things are lawful for me," but not all things are profitable. "All things are lawful for me," but not all things build up. Let no one seek his own, but each one his neighbor's good. **Whatever is sold in the butcher shop, eat, asking no question for the sake of conscience**, for "the earth is the Lord's, and its fullness." But if one of those who don't believe invites you to a meal, and you are inclined to go, eat **whatever is set before you**, asking no questions for the sake of conscience. But if anyone says to you, "**This was offered to idols**," don't eat it for the sake of the one who told you, and for the sake of conscience. For "the earth is the Lord's, with all its fullness." Conscience, I say, not your own, but the other's conscience. For why is my liberty judged by another conscience? If I partake with thankfulness, why am I denounced for something I give thanks for? Whether therefore you eat or drink, or whatever you do, do all to the glory of God. Give no occasion for stumbling, whether to Jews, to Greeks, or to the assembly of God; even as I also please all men in all things, not seeking my own profit, but the profit of the many, that they may be saved."

Paul's counsel here is not an abrogation of the food laws of Leviticus 11. He is teaching about the perception of idolatry and the sensitivities of others. He is referring to buying and eating otherwise Biblical food that may or may not have been offered to idols. He previously stated in 1 Corinthians 8:4 that "that no idol is anything in the world". The issue is the conscience of the other person.

He is saying that if you eat Biblically approved meat sold in the market, don't concern yourself about whether it was used in idolatry. If you go to a meal and are offered meat, Paul says to "eat whatever is set before you, asking no questions for the sake of conscience". He is not saying to eat non-food prohibited by Leviticus 11. The issue is whether this food was sacrificed to idols.

On the other hand, Paul does say, "But if anyone says to you, **"This was offered to idols,"** don't eat it for the sake of the one who told you, and for the sake of conscience." He is teaching the idea of deferring to the sensitivities of another person's conscience. He invokes the ethic of not wanting to cause anyone to stumble, even though he personally knows that "an idol is nothing" and there is nothing wrong with the meat in question.

Galatians 2:11-14

Paul's confrontation with Peter is quite interesting from several angles. Remember in our review of the issues addressed in Acts 10 that Peter had previously struggled with his own prejudice against gentiles based on the man-made traditions that created a strong barrier against any form of table fellowship or interactions with them. This bias was so strong that God had to repeat the vision of Acts 10 to Peter three times and after that, he was still puzzled by it.

At the time of this incident in Antioch, there was still in existence a strong and influential "party of the circumcision" within the struggling Messianic community in Jerusalem. This group was apparently still holding to the man-made traditions of the rabbis that insisted that gentiles had to undergo the ritual conversion ceremony, including circumcision, to "become Jews" in order to be saved. This is the backdrop for the story of Peter here in Antioch. This question was not resolved until the Jerusalem council in Acts 15. That council repudiated this legalism but in no way separated gentiles from torah observance. That was not the issue. Acts 15:1 clearly states what the issue was that they addressed and resolved.

Paul states in the text, "But when Peter came to Antioch, I resisted him to his face, because he stood condemned. For before **some people came from Jacob**, he ate with the Gentiles. But when they came, he drew back and separated himself, **fearing those who were of the circumcision**. And the rest of the Jewish believers joined him in his **hypocrisy** so that even Barnabas was carried away with their **hypocrisy**. But when I saw that they didn't walk uprightly according to the truth of the Good News, I said to Peter before them all, "If you, being a Jew, live as the Gentiles do, and not as the Jews do, why do you compel the Gentiles to live as the Jews do?"

We see here the full measure of how the man-made tradition of separating Jews and gentiles causes so much damage to the body of the Messiah. Paul openly and publicly rebuked Peter because his actions were a public denial of the truth of the gospel message.

I find it interesting that we have recorded this major error by Peter and its subsequent correction by Paul. If, as the Roman Catholic church teaches, Peter was the first "Pope" whose pronouncements on "faith and morals" are "infallible" and "irreformable", then how does that apply here? Peter was clearly not in charge. Actually, Ya'akov, aka Jacob, the Lord's brother, was the leader of the Jerusalem assembly, not Peter. Peter was clearly wrong in his theology regarding gentiles. He was still in bondage to the traditions of men and acted out of fear to the party of the circumcision who had arrived from Jerusalem.

Paul describes this as hypocrisy and says that "even Barnabas was carried away with their hypocrisy". He understood the importance of table fellowship between Jews and gentiles. He likely reflected on Yeshua's words when referring to gentiles in Matthew 8:11, "I tell you that many will come from the east and the west, and will sit down with Abraham, Isaac, and Jacob in the Kingdom of Heaven." It is important to note that this future Messianic banquet will contain Jews and gentiles sitting with each other. There will be one table. There will be one menu and it will be Biblically kosher.

Romans 14

This chapter in Romans is another portion of Scripture frequently cited as "the end of the argument" to show that the food laws of Leviticus 11 have been done away with. Aside from the obvious mistake that would be in light of what Messiah said regarding the Torah in Matthew 5:17-19, let us examine the text piece by piece to learn exactly what Paul is teaching here.

Romans 14:1-4 states, "Now accept one who is **weak in faith**, but not for **disputes over opinions**. One man has faith to eat **all things**, but he who is weak eats **only vegetables**. Don't let him who eats despise him who doesn't eat. Don't let him who doesn't eat judge him who eats, for God has accepted him. Who are you who judge another's servant? To his own lord he stands or falls. Yes, he will be made to stand, for God has power to make him stand."

The first observation is that Paul is referring to "disputes over opinions". That is a telling characterization. Paul is a staunch supporter of the authority of the Torah. All of his teachings and arguments are based upon it. Would the Apostle Paul refer to the Torah of God as "opinions"? Of course not. For Paul, the Torah is absolute and settled. There is no room for challenges there. Paul's "issue" that he was dealing with were "opinions", not settled theology like the Torah.

Secondly, the text informs us that this issue was between people who had faith to eat **all things**, versus those who eat **only vegetables**. This was an issue between the meat eaters and the vegetarians. In fact, these vegetarians were characterized as being "weak in faith". This phrase has been incorrectly applied to believers who eat according to the food laws of Leviticus 11, such as Messianic Jews and Torah-observant gentiles. This is wrong. The people described are vegetarians and there is nothing in the Torah that requires a vegetarian diet. When it comes to the "disputes over "opinions" regarding meat eating versus vegetarianism, Paul's counsel is to not be judgmental but to proceed with grace and tolerance. Good advice!

When we reconcile Paul's words with the rest of the Bible, we avoid "going off page" and twisting Paul's words into something he did not say. If Paul were giving the okay to eat unclean food, it would not be in line with the rest of his teaching or with the end-time prophecy of Isaiah 65 and 66 which relates to God's future judgment on those defiant swine eaters. I guess God cares about Leviticus 11 after all!

The text continues in Romans 14:5,6, "One man esteems **one day as more important**. Another esteems **every day alike**. Let each man be fully assured in his own mind. He who observes the day, observes it to the Lord; and he who does not observe the day, to the Lord he does not observe it. He who eats, eats to the Lord, for he gives God thanks. He who doesn't eat, to the Lord he doesn't eat, and gives God thanks."

These verses have sometimes been misused to try to show that the weekly Shabbat is no longer an issue, that, in fact, it doesn't matter if you keep any of the holy days listed in Leviticus 23. This can hardly be the case since Paul is not referring to the Shabbat. It is not mentioned in the text. Also, that interpretation is impossible in light of Exodus 31:16,17 which states, "Therefore the children of Israel shall keep the Sabbath, to observe the Sabbath **throughout their generations**, for a **perpetual covenant**. It is a sign between me and the children of Israel **forever**;"

What Paul is most likely referring to, based on verse 6, is which day to fast on, something that can be a matter of opinion, but not specified in the Torah.

Paul provides a clear example of grace in dealing with these "disputes over opinions" in Romans 14:13, " Therefore let's not judge one another anymore, but judge this rather, that no man put a stumbling block in his brother's way, or an occasion for falling." This is consistent with Paul's appeal for graciousness in 1 Corinthians 10.

The next verse has also been misunderstood and twisted into an argument against Leviticus 11. Romans 14:14 states, "I know and am persuaded in the Lord Yeshua that **nothing is unclean of itself**; except that to him who considers anything to be unclean, to him it is unclean." Did Paul really mean when saying "nothing is unclean of itself" that there are no unclean foods? Some people say, "Absolutely! That is the end of the argument. No foods are unclean."

One of the problems with Bible translators, as we have seen, is bias. The actual Greek word in the text is "koinos" which means "common", not "unclean". It is a mistranslation to write the text using the word "unclean". That would require the Greek word "akathartos". In the Septuagint, the Greek translation of the Tanach, the word "akathartos" is used when translating the

Hebrew word "tamei" which means "unclean". This is the word used to describe the "unclean" foods of Leviticus 11.

In saying "nothing is common", Paul is not referring to what the Torah has declared as non-food. He is saying that "nothing is common", meaning otherwise Biblically fit food is not rendered unfit for consumption simply by being offered to idols or polluted by idols. This is consistent with his teaching in 1 Corinthians 10.

Concluding Thoughts

In our quest to follow Yeshua in all things and Paul who charged us as well to "imitate me as I imitate Messiah, we should embrace the full weight of Messiah's words in Matthew 5:17-19, "Don't think that I came to destroy the Torah or the Prophets. I didn't come to destroy but to fulfill. For most certainly, I tell you, until heaven and earth pass away, not even one smallest letter or one tiny pen stroke shall in any way pass away from the Torah until all things are accomplished. Therefore, whoever shall break one of these least commandments and teach others to do so, shall be called least in the Kingdom of Heaven; but whoever shall do and teach them shall be called great in the Kingdom of Heaven."

1. This extra-Biblical tradition of men was previously discussed in the chapter on Judaisms.

Chapter Twenty-Seven

Tithes and Offerings

"What does the Bible really <u>SAY?</u>"

Few topics or sermons are as likely to trigger a host of responses, rebuttals, arguments, and psychological defense mechanisms as the subject of money. As human beings, it is a given that we usually feel a little cautious and concerned when others attempt to tell us what we should do with our money. Therein lies part of the problem. Perhaps we should answer the question, "Whose money is it, anyway?"

The following study is designed to assist the thoughtful and reflective reader of Scripture in investigating what the Word of God has to say about the subject of giving. This is not an exhaustive study on money or wealth. It is not specifically an exhortation with an agenda in mind. Rather, it is designed as an interactive guide to help you understand the Word of God and to know how to separate it from the teachings and traditions of men that may be in conflict.

A matter of perspective

We often hear preachers and teachers telling us that the Bible commands us to "tithe" to the congregation. Where do they get this command from? Nowhere in the so-called "New Testament" is there a command to "tithe". That is not to say that giving is not commanded. Tithing is commanded in the Tanach, what Christians call the "Old Testament". It is interesting that the vast majority of evangelical Christians today who reject the applicability and authority of the Torah as God's teaching for His redeemed community will lift this one concept of tithing out and include it in their "statement of faith". This is hardly consistent with the Word of God. The other problems with how "tithes and offerings" are represented to believers will become apparent as we examine what the Scriptures actually say. Please put your emotions on the shelf and be submissive to the absolute authority of the Word of God. It is His source of gracious instruction to His redeemed community.

Here is the challenge:

1. Pray that the Holy Spirit will open your eyes to the Word of God and reveal His truth to you

2. Open your Bible. (I have chosen to not reprint all the Bible passages addressed due to their length.)

3. Read the verses.

4. Write your responses.

5. Consider the conclusions.

What is a tithe?

Genesis 14:18-20

The Hebrew word for "tithe" is ma'aser from the root asar and means "a tenth" or "a grouping of ten". This is the first mention of the tithe in Scripture.

Questions:

- What was the percentage that Abraham used in giving

to Melchizedek?

- What is the basic definition of a "tithe"?

The First Tithe

Leviticus 27:30-33

Questions:

- According to these verses, what is the source of where the tithe comes from?

- Is there any indication that money is being tithed?

- To whom does this tithe belong?

Numbers 18:21-24

Questions:

- Who is the designated recipient of this first tithe given to the LORD?

- According to these verses, what is the source of where the tithe comes from?

- Is there any indication that money is being tithed?

- What is the reason for this tithe being given to these recipients?

- Was this a temporary or a permanent regulation?

- Some would consider that this tithe can be appropriated by modern day "pastors, ministers or congregations". How would you respond according to what these Scriptures explicitly state concerning the specific identity of the recipients?

The Second Tithe

Deuteronomy 14:22-27

Questions:

- According to verse 22, how often was this tithe taken?

- According to these verses, what is the source of where the tithe comes from?

- Is there any indication that money is being tithed?

- According to verse 23, where was this first tithe to be taken?

- Could this tithe be taken just anywhere?

- What was to be done with the tithe?

- How is this different than the first tithe?

- According to verse 27, who else was to share in this tithe?

Deuteronomy 12:4-7

Questions:

- Where was the tithe to be brought?

- Could the tithe be brought just anywhere?

- According to verse 7 what was to be done with the tithe and offering?

- What do you think was the purpose of such an occasion?

The Third Tithe

Deuteronomy 14:28-29

Questions:

- According to verse 28, how often was this tithe taken?

- According to these verses, what is the source of where the tithe comes from?

- Is there any indication that money is being tithed?

- Where was this tithe to be brought?

- Is there anything in these Scriptures that indicate this tithe was to be given in support of the tabernacle?

- What was the intended purpose of this tithe?

- Who were to be the recipients of these tithes?

- What is the anticipated outcome of obedience to these commands?

Deuteronomy 26:12-15

Questions:

- According to verse 12, how often was this tithe taken?

- According to these verses, what is the source of where the tithe comes from?

- Is there any indication that money is being tithed?

- According to verse 12, where was this giving to take place?

- What was the intended purpose of this tithe?

- Who were to be the recipients of these tithes?

- What is the anticipated outcome of obedience to these commands?

A favorite Scripture that is frequently appealed to in modern congregational prayers for "the tithes and offerings" and especially during "pledge drives" or "building projects" is the following:

Malachi 3:10

Questions:
- What is the "storehouse" mentioned here?

- Was the storehouse some kind of local "congregation"?

- Where was this "storehouse" located?

- How often was the third tithe taken?

- What was it that was brought into this storehouse?

- Is there any indication that money is being tithed?

- Where was to be done with this tithe?

- What was the intended purpose of this tithe?

- Who were to be the recipients of these tithes?

- What is the anticipated outcome of obedience to these commands?

- Based upon the previously cited Scriptures, why would it be wrong to assert that this text refers to an annual tithe?

- Why would it be wrong to assert that money was that which was stored in the storehouses?

- Also, why would it be wrong to claim that the modern "congregation" is the storehouse referred to in all the passages describing the third tithe?

What is an offering?

Exodus 25:1-8

Questions:

- The LORD ordered Moshe to take up a collection from the children of Israel to build the Tabernacle. According to verse 2, what was the standard to measure the appropriate amount of "giving"?

- Was the word "tithe" used in connection with this collection?

- Did everyone give the same amount? Why or why not?

- Does anything indicate that there was a limit on how

much one could give?

- Is it possible that some gave more than 10%, a "tithe"?

- What was the stated purpose of all this giving?

- What does this mean for us as we seek to understand the heart attitude that God is seeking among givers?

Exodus 35:4-35

Questions:

- The LORD ordered Moshe to take up a collection from the children of Israel to build the Tabernacle. According to verses 5, 21, 22, 26, and 29 what was the standard to measure the appropriate amount of "giving"?

- Was the word "tithe" used in connection with this collection?

- Did everyone give the same amount? Why or why not?

- Does anything indicate that there was a limit on how much one could give?

- Is it possible that some gave more than 10%, a "tithe"?

- Did everyone have the same "talent" to commit to the building project?

- What does this mean for us as we seek to understand the

heart attitude that God is seeking among givers?

Exodus 36:1-7

Questions:

- What do you make of the fact that God has equipped different people with different gifts and skills in order to get the job done?

- What was the selection criteria of who participated according to verse 2?

- According to verses 3-7, what do we learn about the heart attitude of those giving from the "problem" that was created that Moshe had to address?

- How would you describe the attitude of those who were

giving? Do you get a sense of "compulsion" or "legalism" here?

1 Chronicles 29:1-10

Questions:

- According to verse 2, how much effort did David exert in the building of the Temple?

- According to verse 3, what was the desire of David's heart set upon?

- In that same verse, what level of giving do we see David offering?

- Do you get a sense of "compulsion" or "legalism" in this

sort of giving?

- In the end of verse 5, David asks a question. Describe what you think was the spirit in which this was given:

- How does verse 6 describe the heart attitude of those who gave and what the result was to the whole community?

Proverbs 11:24-25

Questions:

- This advice runs counter to the worldly wisdom that would encourage stinginess and hoarding. What is the outcome for those who keep a tight hold on their wealth?

- What is the outcome for those who consistently bless others?

Proverbs 14:21

Questions:

- What does this teach us about what our attitude should be towards those less fortunate?

- What is the blessing to us as we are compassionate?

Proverbs 19:17

Questions:

- When we give to those in need, to whom are we really blessing?

- What is the outcome to us in response to our kindness towards others?

Proverbs 22:9

Questions:

- How are those who are generous described?

- What is the action that describes such generosity?

Matthew 6:1-4

Questions:

- What is the consequence of a prideful display of one's giving?

- What is the reward they do receive?

- What is the consequence of "secret" giving without public display?

- What is the reward they receive?

I Corinthians 9:8-18

Questions:

- If God is concerned about the provision for cattle, how much more do you think He is concerned about provision for His servants who minister the gospel? Do believers have a responsibility to provide for the needs of their leaders and teachers? How do we provide for this?

- Paul refers to God's provision for the Levites through the tithe. Verse 14 suggests that this provision for ministers of the gospel is "in the same way" as the Levitical tithe but not identical. Since the first tithe was for Levites only and Paul was from the tribe of Benjamin, Paul must be referring to this "right" of provision to be other than the tithe, such as the free-will offerings. Following Paul's example, should leaders and teachers legalistically make demands on those they lead and teach?

1 Corinthians 16:1-4

Questions:

- Paul's counsel regarding collections provides consistency without compulsion. How often does he suggest believers set aside their gifts?

- The first day of every week refers to the ending of the Shabbat at sundown. What does this mean for congregations who insist on taking an offering during the Shabbat?

- Is there any indication that the believers were "tithing" or was this an "offering"?

- According to verse 2, what is the standard to determine the level of giving?

2 Corinthians 8:1-15

Questions:

- The poor believers in Greece had chosen to donate an offering to the poor in Jerusalem. In providing direct relief to those in need, how does this relate to the concept of the "third tithe" mentioned in the Torah?

- According to verse 8, was the need shared as a legalistic demand or was it based upon grace?

- According to verse 11, what was the standard that determined the amount of giving?

- According to verse 15, what is the end result of everyone participating in giving?

2 Corinthians 9:1-15

Questions:

- According to verse 5, a "genuine" gift is not extracted by pressure. What constitutes a "genuine" gift?

- How does this appeal by Paul contrast to modern guilt-inducing and arm-twisting manipulations to "give to get"?

- If believers were giving with a grudging attitude out of compulsion or legalism would their gift still be considered "genuine"?

- According to verse 7, what is the standard to determine how much one should give?

- According to verse 7, what is the right heart attitude of the giver?

- Verse 8 gives us a clue as to one of the reasons God chooses to bless us with provisions. What is it?

- According to verses 11 and 12, what is the ultimate benefit of all this giving?

Luke 18:18-27

Questions:

- Was Yeshua teaching that all believers should sell everything they have and give it all to the poor?

- Why do you suppose that Yeshua's words made this man "very sad"?

- Is it possible that Yeshua was giving a specific targeted prescription to this one individual who obviously had issues with money?

- Do you think the rich man's value and appreciation of money was different than Yeshua's?

- Who do you think have more "money problems", poor people or rich people?

- What is it about wealth that can become a snare for people?

1 Timothy 6:17-19

Questions:

- Paul's counsel to those who are blessed with riches include an admonition to not be proud or to let their hope rest on such wealth. Why could having riches be a trap for genuine humility and trust for the believer?

- Could trusting in one's wealth be a form of idolatry?

- What should be the actions of those who are so blessed?

- If those blessed with riches are generous, what is the anticipated outcome for them?

1 John 3:16-18

Questions:

- When we consider the incomparable and matchless gift that Yeshua gave on our behalf, what does this mean as we contemplate our level of giving to others?

- If we are to "lay down our lives for our brothers", how much more should we be willing to share our worldly goods to help those in real need?

- If we are aware of someone's need and close our heart to responding, what does this say about our claim to love God?

- What does verse 18 mean?

James 1:27

Questions:
- In providing direct relief to those in need, how does this relate to the concept of the "third tithe" mentioned in the Torah?

- How does God view this type of giving?

James 2:14-19

Questions:

- In providing direct relief to those in need, how does this relate to the "third tithe" mentioned in the Torah?

- Do we have a responsibility to our brother or sister? What is it?

- What does it mean to have faith that does not validate itself by outward actions?

- Which is harder, "saying" or "doing"?

- What is more important, creeds or deeds?

Some warnings:

We have all been exposed to some serious errors on the topic of giving.

- We don't "give to get". That is the wrong motivation. It is a significant twisting of the giving principles fueled by base greed.

- We don't give mechanically "out of duty", although we do have a duty to our brothers and sisters.

- God's work is dependent on your giving. Really? What about the sovereignty and omnipotence of God?

Remember the following:

Luke 11:42

Questions:

- What did Yeshua think of those who legalistically give but neglect the justice and love of God?

- Did He say they had an obligation to justice and love?

- Did that mean to neglect giving?

Conclusions:

- If the first tithe was food explicitly for the Levite in the service of the Tabernacle/Temple and had to be presented there, what does that mean for its applicability today when there are no Levites serving in the temple?

- If the second tithe was food to be consumed by the offeror and his family at the temple, what does this mean for its applicability today when there is no temple?

- If the third tithe (taken every third year) was food to be given to the poor in our neighborhoods, how can we accomplish this today?

- In your examination of the Scriptures that describe the three tithes, do you see any evidence that we are to tithe money?

- When you examine all the Scriptures describing "collections" or "offerings", do you see a pattern of giving money, time, talent, and resources?

- In terms of "offerings" and "collections", do you see any limits on what we can give?

- Based upon all the Scriptures you have read, what should determine our level of giving, and what should be our heart attitude?

A closing exercise:

Pray that the Holy Spirit will enlighten you to areas of resistance to giving, areas of legalism in giving, and especially areas of pride in giving. Make a plan to set aside that which God has blessed you with and be diligent in giving out of a cheerful heart.

Always remember that the ultimate "payoff" of our consistent, faithful giving is to the glory of God! May He be praised for His matchless giving of His dear Son as the ultimate gift! If God has given so much to us, how much more should we be ready and eager to give to Him? Praise the Lord!

Chapter Twenty-Eight

The "Holy Protestant Traditions"

As a Messianic Rabbi, when talking with Evangelical Protestants, I oftentimes have some interesting dialogues. Years ago, I was in a Christian bookstore looking for a particular reference. As was my practice, I was wearing my yarmulke, admittedly a man-made tradition but not an anti-biblical one. As I was looking through the books, I noticed two men who kept looking my way. They would exchange glances with each other and then look my way, turning away as soon as I looked at them. I knew they were curious and probably thinking, "What's this Jewish guy doing in here, in a Christian bookstore?" I decided to wander over and engage in a conversation. I commented something like it was a nice bookstore. One of the guys couldn't wait to ask me what I was doing there. I told them I was from a Messianic congregation and that I was a believer in Yeshua, "Jesus" to them, and about the books I was looking for, and then I asked them what they were doing there.

They were quite amazed. This was something unique to their experience. I don't think they ever actually met a Messianic Jew before. (Isn't that a shame?)

One of them told me that they were Bible teachers at a local church and they had just finished a study series with their people and they were looking for something new to start another cycle of teaching. When he said the word "cycle" I immediately thought of the "cycle" of the festivals listed in Leviticus 23. I asked them, "Have you ever considered teaching the cycle of God's festivals in Leviticus 23?" I said, "God set these as Torah teaching pictures that we repeat each year. During this time, we re-experience all of the great history of God's covenant faithfulness to us and also all the great doctrines of our faith as actually lived out. Creation, atonement, deliverance, redemption, sanctification, resurrection, and acceptance with God through the work of Messiah are all pictured, prophesied, and promised to us." These two guys were utterly amazed. One of them said, "I never thought of that." I responded, "It's not an entirely original idea. It's been around for 3,400 years or so" We all laughed and they went away looking for some material I recommended. You see, these two men were stuck in a traditional theology that artificially separates the Bible and its teachings into the camps of "then" for "those people" and "now" for "us". The challenge is to see the entire Word of God as one of continuity instead of contrast.

The story is typical of the modern mindset, especially within most, but not all, Evangelicals. Due in large measure to the rigid compartmentalization of things emanating from the error of Dispensationalism, many view not only the Bible but their interactions with people through this distorted lens that tries to fit everything into the square holes and round holes defined by their theology. As applied to Christian/Jewish definitions, this "binary bias", as I call it, has relegated all expressions and experiences into two camps. Either you are a Christian and go to "church" on Sunday, celebrate Christmas and Easter, and are "saved" or you are a Jew and go to "synagogue" on Saturday and celebrate "all those Jewish festivals" in the "Old Testament". What a shame this thinking has become the norm for so many people within the one body of Messiah. This thinking is also seen outside the realm of Evangelical Christianity.

Another example of a bit of a "paradigm shift" was my interactions with a guy who worked for me at a counseling agency. I hired him and he was a great worker. At first, I did not know he was Jewish. (No, we don't all look alike, and we don't all have the nose of a prophet. That is just a stereotype.) Since I wore my yarmulke, he knew I was. The topic came up one day when he asked me where I attended. I told him the name and shared that it was a Messianic congregation and that I was a believer in Yeshua as Messiah. He was a little shocked but curious since he had seen my demeanor and how I was not aggressive with my faith. I shared that I have a Jewish background but was raised as a Roman Catholic and later rejected that and eventually embraced Messianic Judaism. I could tell he had never encountered anyone with that testimony. I left it at that without pushing any agenda.

Later he came back and asked me about my faith. He was curious and asked, "Do you celebrate Christmas?" I said, "No, but I do embrace Hannukah". He left and, again, I did not push into him. Another time he asked, "What about Easter? Do you celebrate that?" Again, I responded, "No, but we do enjoy the celebration of Passover." He was really curious. Still, I left him alone to ponder things. Another time he asked a few questions and each time I answered him straightforwardly but without any pressure to "buttonhole" him into a corner and start preaching and peppering him with Bible verses. I let him feel that his questions were heard and answered but, most importantly, that he felt safe to return if he had more questions. This, I believe, is the wisdom of being a "fisher of men". We offer bait, we wait and we wait some more. Different bait for different fish, perhaps, but we let them nibble as they wish. I recall someone once said, "Yeshua called us to be fishers of men, not hunters." A lot of wisdom there. A while later this guy invited us to his daughter's Bat Mitzvah at their congregation. My wife and I attended and had a wonderful time. Since he was sitting next to me, he was amazed that during the service we were both praying in Hebrew from the same prayer book. I think he was really stunned by that.

The part of me that is evangelistic would like to finish the story of how he came to faith in the Messiah and became a believer. That is not how this story went. He left the agency, and I never heard any more from him. But I am sure that is not the end of the story for him. Seeds were planted and I leave the rest to God. The main point of my relating this is to show how preconceived bias exists but can be overcome by the right kind of witnessing.

By simply living and acting out my Torah-positive, Messiah-centered, grace-filled faith, I am presenting something in the category of "other" to the world of religious thought. I am not representative of a "typical Jew" if there ever could be such a thing. I am also certainly not representative of a "typical Christian", and we all know there are none of those either. But I am presenting something outside of the normal range of expectations from either camp. Having said that, I immediately realized how sad it is that what was the norm in expression in the first-century Messianic experience has become the oddity.

How far we have divided among ourselves and embraced false teachings and erroneous positions?

The various branches of Protestantism have done this in spades. Much of this is due to branches growing out of other branches and repeating and compounding previous errors. Some have added new errors along the way. Each branch can be traced back to its breaking from some other stream of the teaching of some man. Very little of the content of the branches retains the solid sap from the original trunk of the tree. A good look at Romans 11 might be in order here for the reader.

To show how far man-made traditions have influenced thought, I recall one of my Bible professors at Bible College. He was an elderly, kind gentleman who had much knowledge and wisdom, although we used to spar on several issues. (I say older, but I realize that at this point in my life, I think I am older than he was then!) He once shared that, due to his church background that went all the way back to his childhood, to that day, he had never been to the movies. We were all shocked.

"Never?", we all said in unison. He went on to tell us that his church traditions required them to avoid going to what were then called "picture shows". For his church culture, it was a mark of piety, and they were quite firm about it. He related a little ditty, "We don't smoke, and we don't chew, and we don't go with girls who do!" We discussed some church rules against dancing, although that hardly squares with King David's expressions of joy and what is described in the Psalms. We had a good discussion of traditions that have been used by churches as requirements and markers of spirituality.

Some churches require abstinence from all alcoholic beverages. I find this curious in light of the many Bible verses that are contrary to such an absolute prohibition.

- 1 Timothy 5:23 says, "Be no longer a drinker of water only but use a little wine for your stomach's sake and your frequent infirmities."

- Psalm 104:14,15 says, "He causes the grass to grow for the livestock, and plants for man to cultivate, that he may produce food out of the earth: wine that makes the heart of man glad, oil to make his face to shine, and bread that strengthens man's heart."

Messiah's own example at the wedding in Cana in John 2 is a problem for the anti-alcohol crusade.

On the other hand, the Bible does warn against drunkenness in Ephesians 5:18 and many other places. This issue is one of temperate and moderate use. Apparently, some see things in the "all or nothing" cognitive distortion that develops into a man-made prohibition and they make this a requirement for membership with their church.

These extra man-made traditions are not a part of the gospel message at all but by their insistent requirement for church membership and continued discipleship, the net effect is to "add to the Word of God". I do not mean to assert their intent is bad. I do not believe the intent of the rabbis who put "fences around the Torah" was necessarily bad either. But is it not the same? And where does it stop?

I have received much praise from Evangelical Protestants over the years for my firm stance on the inspiration and authority of the Scriptures, my continued appeal of "sola Scriptura", meaning only the Scriptures are our authority and not the Oral Torah of the rabbis, the church councils, or pronouncements of the popes. But I find it interesting that when my focus is on the many man-made traditions that I find within the large umbrella of Protestantism, including some Messianic congregations, the praise quickly dissipates into suspicion and distrust. I have often experienced "the left boot of fellowship". It just shows how deeply entrenched these traditions have become.

Chapter Twenty-Nine

The Stages of Change

H ow many counselors does it take to change a light bulb? Only one, but the light bulb has to want to change.

Over my 30 years of clinical experience in counseling and education, I have learned many things. Some have been useful to me, others have not. Over the years, it was revealed to me that there are major discrepancies between many of the theories and traditions of modern psychology and the sure and steadfast witness of the Bible.

I was initially educated in Freudian psychoanalysis, Transactional Analysis by Harris and Steiner, Client-Centered therapy by Carl Rogers, Behaviorism and Operant Conditioning by B.F. Skinner, Self-Actualization by Abraham Maslow, Reality Therapy by William Glasser, Gestalt Therapy by Fritz Perls, and various Encounter Groups and Sensitivity Trainings, including much early "New Age" teachings. You have to know that back in the 1970s if you weren't in therapy, you were in denial!

You can imagine my confusion! This was all BEFORE I became a believer and began understanding the Bible.

Since becoming a believer in 1976 and having learned what the Bible teaches, I have thrown overboard most of the humanistic "Psycho-babble", as I refer to it. During my walk with the Lord, I have learned many things, some that were easy to understand and embrace, some that were more difficult. I learned from the Bible that the central issues of what is wrong with man are NOT his "nature and environment", "irrational thinking", "cultural lag", "class struggle", "human weakness and ignorance", or "primitive instinct left over from evolution." The Bible calls it SIN and there is only ONE remedy and that is the once-for-all sacrifice of Yeshua and the continuing ministry of the Holy Spirit within.

All through this process, I have been guided by His Spirit speaking through His Word. I am not yet a finished product. There remains more work to be done. That is called progressive sanctification and I embrace it fully, trusting in His wise and loving care for me.

One of the constructs that I learned through education and training and have personally validated through observation and experience was the value and application of what is called the "Stages of Change", also known as the "Transtheoretical Model". Although emanating from the field of psychology and counseling, I have found this understanding to be in harmony with and not opposed to Biblical truth and very effective in helping others make significant and lasting changes in their own lives. I offer my take on this as a useful approach in counseling and discipling others. The initial task is to explain the concept and its application to our tasks as people helpers. I will conclude with Biblical examples of how this actually plays out in our interactions with people. I do not want anyone to receive this teaching as a "formula approach" or "canned sales pitch". It is not a rigid method. It is helpful to see this as a "flow" that is useful to understanding the complexities of the processes involved. It is provided with the understanding that true Biblical counsel will always be centered on the Word of God and dependent on the leading and inspiration of the Holy Spirit as He brings conviction and enlightenment into the soul of man.

How to Help People

The first rule of helping is simple: DO NO HARM.

Ephesians 4:29 says, "Let no corrupt speech proceed out of your mouth, but only what is good for building others up as the need may be, that it may give grace to those who hear."

We don't need a dictionary to inform us of the meaning of the word corrupt. We see examples in the news every day. Aside from its description of political power grabs, unlawful business practices, and personal moral failures, it can also describe falsehoods, untruths, lies, deceit, and errors. The text here in Ephesians should remind us to guard what we say in terms of truthfulness. I believe the best way to ensure our words are based on truth is that they are based on the Word of God, the source of ultimate truth.

Our speech is also directed to be only that which is good for building others up, not tearing them down. In our approach to helping people, there is simply no room for personal attacks, put-downs, manipulations, or self-serving hypocrisy.

Finally, our words should always be seasoned with grace. It is by grace WE have been saved, so we need to extend that to all others as well.

It is especially important that we understand that we can be correct in our theology and wrong in our approach. I have seen, and been a victim of, many "fleshly" arguments from well-meaning people, who may say correct things, but their spirit causes defensiveness, confusion, and rejection.

I reject "canned" sales-track approaches to evangelism and counseling. They tend to pigeonhole people's issues and concerns into categories to then attempt to refute them. I think some of the so-called "witnessing" methods and approaches tend to appeal to the pride and showmanship of the witness rather than a genuine, in-depth exploration into the needs of the individual. I remember back in 1970 as a young man, not yet a believer, being witnessed to by a number of "Jesus Freaks" as they were called. I had rejected Catholicism, as I mentioned previously, but did not have a suitable replacement for the content of my faith. I had a lot of sincere questions. I was interested in what these believers apparently possessed, and I did have some dialogues with them. My discussions, however well-intentioned on their part, were much more of a hindrance to my understanding than true help. When I asked numerous questions, I was met with a barrage of Bible verses, almost always in King James English, which I do not speaketh. When responding for clarification, yet more Bible verses came my way. I finally stopped dialoguing altogether in frustration at not understanding. It took another 6 years for me to discover the meaning and truth of the Word of God. How sad that a genuine seeker of His truth should experience so many barriers to that truth.

The above verse from Ephesians contains the important clause about "building others up as the need may be". It is this discovery of the unique issues and needs within the individual and tailoring our responses to those issues that make our counsel effective.

Exercise #1

Let's examine our own history with changes we have made to gain a better understanding of the stages of change.

What fears, concerns, and expectations do you have when you consider encouraging others to change a particular position in terms of theology? Many people, if not most, will honestly list fear of rejection, perhaps anger and fleshly argumentation, failure to "get the point across", or even loss of friendship. Many simply refrain from interaction on certain subjects, such as "sex, politics, and religion", to keep the peace. We become timid and tied to our fears, oftentimes related to our past ineffectual and frustrating attempts to counsel others.

So, let's try to understand how the process works by a little personal reflection.

- Think of some particular theological position that you have successfully changed in your past. It could be what

faith means, what salvation means, any particular doctrine or teaching, or understanding of a Bible verse.

- Now consider how much time elapsed between your
  original position on the subject and when you realized some discrepancy between your previous belief and
  what the Bible teaches. For many, this gap of time could
  be months or even years. It took time to recognize and
  appreciate the subtleties and nuances of context. Some
  of us spent much time simply living with this unresolved question.

- Now consider how much time elapsed between the very
  first time you recognized this discrepancy between your
  belief and the Bible and the first time you made an
  earnest attempt to reconcile the issue. Again, this gap
  of time could be months or years.

- Finally, consider how much time elapsed between your
  first attempt at changing your position and the time
  when you resolved all your questions and fully embraced your new position. Again, likely to be months
  or years.

The Progression of Change

In the above example, we see the progression of change as we moved between the following:

- Your original position.

- First awareness of a discrepancy between your belief and the Bible.

- First attempt to change your position.

- Final resolution of issues and questions and fully embrace the new position.

Now, let's ask some tougher questions about the above exercise.

- Did you ever experience some success in changing your position?

- Did you ever experience hesitation or confusion?

- Did you ever experience a return to your original position after experiencing some success at changing it?

Conclusions drawn from this exercise:

- Theological challenges are common.

- Change often takes a long time. We go through periods of searching, wondering, exploring, seeking advice, or studying.

- The pace of change is variable. We may make rapid progress in our understanding one day and slow down to barely any the next.

- Knowledge is usually not sufficient to motivate and complete change. It is not always a "gang of facts" that convinces us. We need to process the ramifications of accepting a new theory.

- Movement is not always linear. Sometimes it's the old "one step forward and two steps backward" experience. We are subject to theological relapse. Change is not usually a binary event. It is not like flipping a light switch.

- Oftentimes, our emotions get in the way. Our confusion and uncertainty about a particular idea create an emotional pull back to the safe waters of the harbor that we know. Fear of the uncertain or unknown with all its possible ramifications can cause us to turn the boat around and head back to shore.

- When we apply these understandings of our own personal experience with change, we can now perhaps begin to understand how our own expectations of other people regarding theological change are frequently unrealistic. As I have taught many new counselors, having unrealistic expectations for other people, no matter how noble or pure the intention or goal, can lead to frustration and burnout.

Exercise #2

- Think about the issue you dealt with in Exercise #1.

- Think about people who were **NOT** helpful to you. How did they come across? What did they do that was **NOT** helpful?

  ○ Judgmental

- Accusing

- Impatient

- Know-it-all superiority

- Condescending

- Unforgiving

- Now, think about people who **WERE** helpful to you. How did they come across? What did they do that **WAS** helpful?

  - Patient

  - Kind

  - Empathic

  - Genuinely Caring

  - Loving

  - Knowledgeable

  - Humble

We can learn from our own experiences with people interacting with us what is helpful and what is not. We can appreciate the need to have more realistic expectations for people in terms of the time needed to process change. We can hopefully appreciate and recognize small "baby steps" as people continue to process. We can have more opportunities for dialogue as people feel safe to continue interacting with us without fear of harsh responses or judgmental disapproval. We can avoid the trap of "all or nothing" thinking which misses the process entirely and demands submission to our will instead of assisting a person to discover the truth for themselves through the process.

I repeat our starting verse:

Ephesians 4:29 says, "Let no corrupt speech proceed out of your mouth, but only what is good for building others up as the need may be, that it may give grace to those who hear."

Motivation and Resistance

As we explore the various stages of change and seek to understand what our role is in each stage, there is one important thing for us to understand as it undergirds the entire process.

There is an inversely proportional relationship between motivation and resistance. What does this mean? Aside from sounding profound, it simply means that when you feel attacked or challenged by someone, it is normal to get defensive. We put the wall up, sometimes even draw the bridge over the moat, and stay secure in our castle. Our motivation to listen and consider a position contrary to what we currently hold goes down or even disappears if we feel threatened by another opinion. It is oftentimes reflexive and unthinking. Sometimes the person offering the opinion or teaching can be as kind and well-meaning as possible, but the results will be the same. The reaction of defensiveness exists within the person whose position is being challenged. Defense mechanisms are internal to us all. They are not always bad, but they usually operate below the surface. They are not designed to trick others. They are designed to protect us.

The way to move forward through the minefield of defense mechanisms is to not directly attack the point of resistance but to focus on the motivations, benefits, and blessings of the new position being advocated. When people begin to cognitively appreciate and embrace the positive feelings associated with the new teaching or doctrine, their defenses relax, and a spark of motivation can begin the journey forward. It is this internal motivation, the intrinsic motivation of attraction, that fans the flame of desire to at least consider embracing the new idea.

I spent most of my counseling career working with court-mandated criminal offenders who only ever attended the prescribed counseling and treatment programs because the judge, probation, and/or parole officers mandated it. Talk about defense mechanisms in full play! The clients were only present because of what is called "extrinsic motivation". If they failed to attend, they were heading to jail, fines, etc. This external motivation was not "change" as I would define it. It was "compliance", which is not the same thing.

The approach I used and taught other counselors was to use this "extrinsic motivation" to keep them involved while we attempted to tap into the "internal motivation" of change to produce movement towards "low-risk choices" and away from "high-risk choices". Having an understanding of how to do this was essential to seeing the many successes with an admittedly difficult population. The same processes are no different for any group of people when dealing with any issue.

There are important distinctions between empathy, sympathy, and compassion. Empathy is the sense that you can understand what another person is feeling and perhaps even why they are feeling it. It is that sense that gives us the perspective of what it's like to "walk in their shoes". Empathy is a one-to-one connection that can be powerful in helping people, as long as they perceive that it is genuine and sincere. Sympathy is more of an emotional reaction like feeling sorry or pity for someone, to actually feel the same thing as they feel. It can lead to emotionalism and away from objectivity. Compassion is more of a general attitude towards people with problems. It is a heart attitude and willingness to help people out of pure motivation.

The Stages of Change

It is helpful to understand that as we interact with people during this process, we "wear different hats", so to speak, depending on where the person is at. Our interactions should never be a scripted, "sales track" that is designed to corner and manipulate someone. There is an old saying that says, "A man convinced against his will is of the same opinion still."

The goal is where someone gets to the point where they say, "God said it. I believe it. That settles it." Much of what is called "witnessing" begins at this point. We need to remember that this is the goal, not the starting point. We get there through a process.

Having established some of the challenges and some suggestions, let's move to an understanding of each stage of change and see what our role is to be in each one.

The Stage of Pre-Contemplation

This first stage of the stages of change is descriptive of position rather than any movement. In fact, there is no movement at all! It describes where a person is at **BEFORE** any movement is even contemplated, thus, Pre-Contemplation. It describes where many people are at with respect to many ideas or concepts. They are simply **NOT** thinking about changing. There are many reasons why people are in this category with respect to changing anything at all. People oftentimes spend months and years stuck in place, so to speak.

- **Reveling**

  - "I am having too much fun with my present belief. It fits my needs. For me, it is "settled theology". I see no need to change."

- **Reluctance**

○ "Change takes too much effort. What difference does it make, anyway? What would others think? If I think of the logical conclusion to what you are saying, it makes me feel uncomfortable or induces fear."

- **Rebellion**

  ○ "I am not teachable. I already know the answer and you're wrong." This demonstration of pride, arrogance, and fleshly ego can be defended with much energy and passion.

- **Resignation**

  ○ "I feel hopeless and overwhelmed by it all. I'll just stay where I am in safety."

- **Rationalizing**

  ○ "I have reasons and answers for everything."

Our Role: Nurturing Parent

- We acknowledge the person's concerns. This is where

empathy comes in. If people think that they are being "heard", that we are really listening and understanding them, we go a long way towards helping them.

- We introduce ambivalence, known in the world of psychology as "cognitive conflict". This is precisely NOT telling them where they are wrong and then telling them what the answer is. This practice causes an almost universal reaction of the person shutting down. The wall goes up, the bridge withdraws, and the castle is safe from the invaders. Much of what is called "witnessing" falls under this description with predictable results.

- When I think of introducing ambivalence, I think of Tevya in "Fiddler on the Roof" who, in his prayers and discussions with God, would frequently say, "On the one hand ... but on the other hand ..." It is a way of not discounting what they are saying but introducing another plausible thought in somewhat of a fair-minded competition. It is critical to understand that the person has to resolve this conflict. We don't do it for them. It is their struggle to resolve and, when they do, they can own it. It takes a little patience, but we need to remember that "we can't push a chain". We develop this discrepancy as skillfully as we can and discuss the concept of change. Not push. Just discuss.

The Stage of Contemplation

The stage of contemplation is when someone BEGINS to think about change. It is not change. It is thinking about change. Since introducing the seed of doubt to someone in pre-contemplation, the seed is allowed to grow and mature. The person begins thinking about it. The chief characteristic of someone in this stage is active ambivalence. They are thinking and processing all the ramifications of the idea.

Our Role: Socratic Method

- Rabbis and many Law and Philosophy professors are known for using the time-honored teaching method of engaging students with open-ended questions, instead of long fact-filled lectures. As an example, ask a Rabbi a question and you will likely get a question back! They want their students to think and process and interactively engage rather than just being a mere sponge soaking up facts and figures.

- We may have open discussions about the options without pressure either way.

- My favorite tool to employ at this point is known as "Decisional Balancing".

Decisional Balancing

I usually engage people with a four-boxed "window pane" on paper with a pencil.

- Pros in favor of the new position.

- Cons against the new position.

- Pros in favor of the old position.

- Cons in favor of the old position.

The idea behind this exercise is to help people fairly represent all sides of the idea, without bias, acknowledging the perceived pros and cons. It is important to not "lean on the scale" in favor of an opinion. Remember, the person has to resolve this to their own satisfaction. As soon as they perceive we are on "one side" they will instinctively react by defending the other. Remember, if defensiveness goes up, motivation to change goes down.

I have used this exercise for many years in private counseling and have seen it work wonders. I have also used this in group counseling and have seen it work with great power and conviction, especially as groups have power and synergy all their own. I have seen many people move rather dramatically from anger and denial through contemplation and into major life decisions in relatively short periods of time. This has sometimes happened during a single therapeutic setting.

The Stage of Planning

Once a person makes a decision as a result of this decisional balancing and decides to go forward, the process has an important step, oftentimes overlooked. The person needs to learn new information. They may need to make new plans. or investigate what traditions to follow. They may be asking, "How do I do it right?"

Our Role: Coach

Enter the coach. We offer support for the motivation to change, perhaps the word growth would be a useful term. We answer questions and provide instructions. We are sitting next to them on the bench cheering them on and providing support. We encourage action and commitment to the ongoing process.

The Stage of Action

There is an overt change of view. The person begins starting new observances or practices. There is a stopping of old practices and continued learning.

Our Role: Consultant

We continue to offer further training, resources, and answers to questions that arise. We recognize that people never stop learning. We continue to support the new changes and reaffirm their commitment to them. We are a source of affirmation and fellowship.

The Stage of Maintenance

This is not so much a stage as the final culmination of the process. It represents sustained change over time. The new theology or practice has become an intrinsic part of the new lifestyle of thinking and doing.

Our Role: Consultant

Our role as a consultant is maintained to reaffirm commitment. The need for continued contact at this point recognizes the reality that sometimes people are subject to theological relapse. A person in any stage can move to a former stage. It is not always a direct, linear path toward acceptance and fully embracing and practicing new ideas or concepts.

Helping people process through these stages of change is part science and facts, part art and intuition, and 100% sensitivity to the Holy Spirit.

What does the Bible say about our attitude and conduct throughout these processes?

- Proverbs 15:18 says, "A wrathful man stirs up contention, but one who is slow to anger appeases strife."

  - It is imperative that in our interactions with others, we remain calm and non-reactive.

- Proverbs 20:3 says, "It is an honor for a man to keep aloof from strife, but every fool will be quarreling."

  - We don't "argue" people into our position.

- Proverbs 26:21 says, "As coals are to hot embers, and wood to fire, so is a contentious man to kindling strife.:

  - Aggression has no place in our witness.

- 1 Corinthians 13:4-7 says, "Love is patient and is kind. Love doesn't envy. Love doesn't brag, is not proud, doesn't behave itself inappropriately, doesn't seek its own way, is not provoked, takes no account of evil; doesn't rejoice in unrighteousness, but rejoices with the truth; bears all things, believes all things, hopes all things, and endures all things."

- We don't "keep score" of past wrongs.

- We don't play the "gotcha game".

- There is no room for unforgiveness, bitterness, or resentment.

- We affirm every positive move, no matter how small.

- Proverbs 29:22 says, "An angry man stirs up strife, and a wrathful man abounds in sin."

  - Anger has no place in our witness.

- Proverbs 30:33 says, "For as the churning of milk produces butter, and the wringing of the nose produces blood, so the forcing of wrath produces strife."

  - No "bloody noses", literal or otherwise.

- Colossians 3:12,13 says, "Put on therefore, as God's chosen ones, holy and beloved, a heart of compassion, kindness, lowliness, humility, and perseverance; bearing with one another, and forgiving each other, if any man has a complaint against any; even as Messiah forgave you, so you also do."

  - This is quite a high standard for forgiveness.

- ○ It is interesting that the Hebrew word for "compassion" is Rachamim. It is always written in the plural which gives us an indication of how extensive God views it.

- Colossians 3:14-16 says, "Above all these things, walk in love, which is the bond of perfection. And let the peace of God rule in your hearts, to which also you were called in one body, and be thankful. Let the word of Messiah dwell in you richly; in all wisdom teaching and admonishing one another with psalms, hymns, and spiritual songs, singing with grace in your heart to the L ord."

  - ○ The content of our counsel is the Word of God.

  - ○ We need to genuinely live it.

  - ○ If you are a faithful believer, if you know His Word, and if you are Spirit-led, then you are qualified to teach and counsel each other.

- Ephesians 4:2,3 says, "With all lowliness and humility, with patience, bearing with one another in love, being eager to keep the unity of the Spirit in the bond of peace."

- Romans 14:1 says, "Now accept one who is weak in faith, but not for disputes over opinions."

- Romans 14:19 says, "So then, let's follow after things which make for peace, and things by which we may build one another up."

  ○ Many things are peripheral, non-essential issues.

  ○ Traditions that are not in conflict with the Word of God are optional. They should never be misused in a legalistic fashion.

- Proverbs 27:9 says, "Perfume and incense bring joy to the heart; so does earnest counsel from a man's friend."

- Proverbs 27:17 says, "Iron sharpens iron; so a man sharpens his friend's countenance."

Consider the Example of Yeshua's Witnessing

- Yeshua called us to be fishers of men, not hunters.

  ○ We have different bait for different fish.

- We go to where the fish are.

- We are patient.

- John 3:16 is not a rifle caliber. It is not a hunting tool.

- Yeshua was compassionate and faithful to the Torah.

  - Matthew 9:36 says, "But when he saw the multitudes, he was moved with compassion for them because they were harassed and scattered, like sheep without a shepherd."

  - Matthew 5:17 says, "Don't think that I came to destroy the Torah or the Prophets. I didn't come to destroy, but to fulfill."

  - Truth without compassion is cruelty.

  - Compassion without truth is co-dependence.

Consider the Woman at the Well

- John 4:1-6 says, "Therefore when the Lord knew that the Pharisees had heard that Yeshua was making and immersing more disciples than Yochanan (although Yeshua himself didn't immerse, but his disciples), he left Judea and departed into Galilee. He needed to pass through Samaria. So he came to a city of Samaria called Sychar, near the parcel of ground that Jacob gave to his son Joseph. Jacob's well was there. Yeshua therefore, being tired from his journey, sat down by the well. It was about the sixth hour."

- ○ Yeshua was not afraid to go outside the established cultural and religious boundaries set by the traditions of men.

- ○ Neither should we.

- John 4:7-10 says, "A woman of Samaria came to draw water. Yeshua said to her, "Give me a drink." For his disciples had gone away into the city to buy food. The Samaritan woman therefore said to him, "How is it that you, being a Jew, ask for a drink from me, a Samaritan woman?" (For Jews have no dealings with Samaritans.) Yeshua answered her, "If you knew the gift of God, and who it is who says to you, 'Give me a drink,' you would have asked him, and he would have given you living water."

- ○ Yeshua was not afraid to openly speak with a Samaritan, especially a Samaritan woman, something Jews of His day would avoid out of prejudice.

- ○ Yeshua did not rebuke the woman for being a Samaritan or for questioning his motives. He did not get defensive.

- ○ His careful interactions were designed to show empathy and love throughout the conversation.

- • John 4:11-14 says, "The woman said to him, "Sir, you have nothing to draw with, and the well is deep. So where do you get that living water? Are you greater than our father Jacob[1], who gave us the well and drank from it himself, as did his children and his livestock?" Yeshua answered her, "Everyone who drinks of this water will thirst again, but whoever drinks of the water that I will give him will never thirst again; but the water that I will give him will become in him a well of water springing up to eternal life."

  - ○ Yeshua took the opportunity to take an ordinary, mundane task of drinking water and transform it into a learning moment. In studying His parables, He did the same thing with ordinary, familiar concepts such as "the lost sheep", "the lost coin", "the prodigal son", "new cloth on an old coat", "new wine in old wineskins", "a lamp on a stand", "wise and foolish builders", "the types of soils", "yeast", "the mustard seed", "the fishing net", etc. The many examples of Yeshua's transforming common everyday experiences that all could relate to and then engaging people to pause and consider deeper spiritual meanings are examples of His mastery of connecting with people.

- This planting of the seed regarding the water carried a deeper spiritual meaning. It caused the woman to ponder the issue. She now had a deeper issue to grasp and reckon with.

- John 4:15-18 says, "The woman said to him, "Sir, give me this water, so that I don't get thirsty, neither come all the way here to draw." Yeshua said to her, "Go, call your husband, and come here." The woman answered, "I have no husband." Yeshua said to her, "You said well, 'I have no husband,' for you have had five husbands; and he whom you now have is not your husband. This you have said truly."

- Yeshua sensitively brought up the issue of her past

husbands and her current relationship.

- ○ It is important that we do not read sarcasm or harsh judgmentalism in His tone. I believe He was full of compassion and patience as he broached the subject.

- ○ She had related high values in her life as she demonstrated respect for her heritage through Jacob and affirmed the Torah's history.

- ○ Yeshua planted the seed of the discrepancy between her values and the realities of her lifestyle without a confrontational style involving harsh disapproval or shaming.

- John 4:19-22 says, "The woman said to him, "Sir, I perceive that you are a prophet. Our fathers worshiped in this mountain, and you Jews say that in Jerusalem is the place where people ought to worship." Yeshua said to her, "Woman, believe me, the hour is coming when neither in this mountain nor in Jerusalem will you worship the Father. You worship that which you don't know. We worship that which we know; for salvation is from the J ews."

- ○ The woman was certainly accurate in describing

Yeshua as a prophet. How else could He know her background?

○ It is interesting that the woman immediately changed the subject to a discussion of the place of worship instead of her current relationship issue. In psychology, this is called deflection. It is not uncommon when we get close to issues, that people's defense mechanisms kick in automatically. When we perceive this in others, it can be a clue that our message has been on track. It is always wise to observe reactions and to think through the why of those reactions to guide us in our dialogue. Counseling others is not a mechanical process. It requires listening to the other person as well as listening to the Holy Spirit.

○ When confronted by the discrepancy between her values and her conduct, she remained ambivalent for a time. This is common. We should not step in to try to resolve the conflict. It is the person who has to process through the discrepancy.

• John 4:23-26 says, "But the hour comes, and now is, when the true worshipers will worship the Father in spirit and truth, for the Father seeks such to be his worshipers. God is spirit, and those who worship him must worship in spirit and truth." The woman said to him, "I know that Messiah is coming, he who is called Messiah. When he has come, he will declare to us all things." Yeshua said to her, "I am he, the one who speaks t o you."

○ It is critical to see that Yeshua continued to paint the picture of true worship and presented ideas about qualifications for worship. He was illustrating the pros of this new understanding of worship. He did not argue with her about her ambivalence. He did not rebuke her or shame her. He allowed her time and space to reflect. His compassionate interactions are a witness to us. His manner and tone continued with respect.

○ He accepted her genuine faith in a coming Messiah.

○ It was at this point that He revealed Himself to her.

• John 4:27-30 says," Just then, his disciples came. They marveled that he was speaking with a woman; yet no one said, "What are you looking for?" or, "Why do you speak with her?" So the woman left her water pot, went away into the city, and said to the people, "Come, see a man who told me everything that I have done. Can this be the Messiah?" They went out of the city, and were coming to him.

- ○ This courageous woman of faith was transformed into a powerful witness to her entire village.

- ○ She had begun in pre-contemplation and was now in the action stage as she was convinced of the truthfulness of her new understanding regarding the Messiah.

• John 4:39-42 says, "From that city many of the Samaritans believed in him because of the word of the woman, who testified, "He told me everything that I have done." So when the Samaritans came to him, they begged him to stay with them. He stayed there two days. Many more believed because of his word. They said to the woman, "Now we believe, not because of your speaking; for we have heard for ourselves, and know that this is indeed the Messiah, the Savior of the world."

- ○ He exhibited empathy and respect throughout the interchange.

- ○ He avoided direct arguments and challenges.

- He sowed the seed of the discrepancy between her values and the realities of her lifestyle.

- He added depth and color to His message to aid in her decisional balancing.

- Yeshua stayed focused on the issue and allowed the woman time and space to process her issues herself toward acceptance of His message.

- He offered Himself as her Messiah.

A Final Word about Our Approach to People

I want to close this section with a poem given to me about 40 years ago or so. I used to have this in a frame on my desk as a constant reminder of the values I have come to embrace. I do not know the identity of the author, or I would certainly give credit. I DO know that the author of this poem knows the Author of our faith!

The harvest is so great, Lord. And the workers, there are few. Help me every chance I get to bring a soul to You.

Fill me with the Spirit, Lord, that I may spread Your Word.

And bring Your hope and joy to those who haven't heard.

There are so many troubled, Lord, so burdened and distressed.

Help me guide them home to You so that they may find their rest.

They are fighting such a battle, a battle they can't win.

Unless they turn to You, Lord, and invite you to come in.

The time is short to labor and the fruit is there to yield.

Guide me in Thy battle, the sword of truth to wield.

You have given me so much, Lord, may I not use it just for me.

But share it with another so that he too may be free.

---

1. Samaritans were half-breeds of Jewish and gentile peoples.

Chapter Thirty

Concluding thoughts

I retired from the counseling profession as a clinical director of counseling programs for criminal offenders with over 30 years of experience in individual and group counseling and teaching. I am quite skilled at reading people. When certain subjects are brought up, no matter how gracefully, I can watch the body language and see the wall come up. People get defensive and, sometimes, they don't even know why. I believe it all goes back to their "settled theology" and "comfortable traditions". We tend to like things the way they are and we don't like change. I think the only people who actually like "change" are wet babies. The rest of us, not so much.

The power of traditions to hold us captive to rigid thinking, legalistic requirements, and intense preoccupation with minutiae was clearly seen in the example we began with in Mark 7 with the Pharisees and their obsessions with ritual hand washing "according to the traditions of the elders". Believers study this and other similar passages and often remark on the erroneous thinking and practices of these Pharisees. How often, however, do they themselves go down similar paths with their own set of man-made traditions and impose them on others with the same level of rigid and inflexible thinking? How often are they themselves in bondage to false ideas about God and His Word that come from the mouths of false teachers "within the church"? I could go down and catalog the various errors of all the false teachers and false prophets just in our current generation alone. That task is way outside the scope of this book, and it would take years to compile. That fact alone makes me sad.

It is important to remember that traditions may be useful if we keep things in proper perspective. If the tradition does not violate the Word of God, it may be appropriate and give us an opportunity to demonstrate our unity in practice. If, however, it does violate the Word of God, it is definitely not appropriate. Just like the "fences around the Torah" created by the rabbis, it is not a sin for not adhering to a tradition. It's just a tradition. The only authoritative, eternal, inspired body of Truth for us to embrace for our faith and practice is the Word of God. The whole Word of God, from Genesis through Revelation. It is all from our Heavenly Father and it is all for our good!

Bibliography and Recommended Reading

Berkowitz, Ariel and D'vorah. Torah Rediscovered, 5th ed. Richmond MI: Shoreshim Publishing, 2011. Available at Amazon.

Berkowitz, Ariel and D'vorah. Take Hold: Embracing Our Divine Inheritance with Israel. 3rd ed. Richmond MI: Shoreshim Publishing. Available at Amazon.

Egan, Hope. Holy Cow! Does God Care About What We Eat? Available at Amazon.

Flores, See-El. Judaism in a Nutshell: The Jewish Calendar

Frydland, Rachmiel. What the Rabbis Know About the Messiah 3rd ed. Available at Amazon.

Hegg, Tim. Fellow Heirs - Jews and Gentiles Together in the Family of God. Available at Amazon and www.torahresource.com

Hegg, Tim. Article titled My Big, Fat, Greek Mindset at www.torahresource.com

Hegg, Tim. The Letter Writer. Available at Amazon and www.torahresource.com

Hegg, Tim. Article titled Why I Don't Celebrate Christmas at www.torahresource.com

Hislop, Alexander. The Two Babylons, 7th ed. Available at Amazon.

Liguori, Cardinal St. Alphonsus. The Glories of Mary. Translated from the Italian. Available at Amazon.

McDowell, Josh. Evidence That Demands a Verdict. Available at Amazon.

The History Channel. The History of Christmas

Wilson, Marvin R. Our Father Abraham: Jewish Roots of the Christian Faith. Available at Amazon.

World Messianic Bible. It is copyright-free and in the public domain. The World Messianic Bible has also been known as the Hebrew Names Version (HNV) and the World English Bible: Messianic Edition (WEB:ME).

Author Bio

I have a vast and varied experience, beginning with a 16-year active-duty career in the United States Navy where I served in many capacities including Avionics, Electronic Warfare, and Espionage systems. I did many tours overseas including having served at Danang Air Base, Vietnam. I then shifted gears and became trained and certified to work in the U.S. Navy's Counseling and Assistance Centers for the majority of my active-duty time. During this period, I was privileged to provide meaningful and in-depth counseling and education to fellow service members struggling with many issues.

After leaving the military, I added several professional certifications as a counselor, instructor, and clinical supervisor and worked in several community counseling agencies. I eventually became a clinical director of counseling programs for criminal offenders and was on a county and state board. Additionally, I have volunteered as a Mentor with a local Veteran's court to provide guidance and direction to other fellow veterans.

Over the course of many years of study, I was ordained as a Messianic Jewish Rabbi in 2013 at Congregation Bet Shalom v'Emet in Fresno, California under the authority of Rabbi Amnon Shor. He is a native-born Israeli with dual citizenship here in the U.S. His knowledge of Hebrew, the Bible, and the many intricacies of Judaism is amazing. I was blessed to have had the opportunity to study and learn under such a great leader in the Messianic movement. If you ever have the opportunity to visit his congregation in Fresno, California, I personally guarantee you will be blessed beyond measure, challenged in your understanding of the Bible, and filled with a greater appreciation of the Jewish heritage of the faith in Messiah Yeshua. His website is www.betshalomfresno.org. Additionally, he is also on YouTube.

Made in the USA
Las Vegas, NV
01 November 2023

79872977R00167